POEM

BY

AN OLD CODGER

Reflective Poems from

World War 2 to COVID-19

with

Observational Poems

From Modern Life

NEIL DAVIES

Published by Independent Publishing Network

Email: info@ipubnet.co.uk

Printed by Book Printing UK www, bookprintinguk.com

Remus House, Coltsfoot Drive, Peterborough, PE2 9BF

Printed in Great Britain

ISBN 978-1-83853-810-1

To all readers,

Welcome to the reflections on the 'seven stages' of my life and the world I have witnessed and lived through for over fourscore years and more.

I hope it brings back memories to those of you of similar age and offers a brief insight for younger readers of our life and times.

"You were not born rich, lad, but I think you were born lucky." My mother's analysis. I have enjoyed a life which has been both rich and lucky, and I am indebted to my wife and my wonderful family and friends for their love, support, and tolerance of this old codger.

Stay safe.

Author

"Life can only be understood backwards,

But it has to be lived forward."

Danish philosopher, Soren Kierkegaard (1813 – 1855)

Foreword

As I move through my four score years, I guess that my compatriots and I owe our children, our grandchildren and our great grandchildren a huge apology for allowing our world to become not as we found it when we came into this life.
We have poisoned the land, the seas, and the air. In so many ways we have reached for the stars whilst killing off our own star.

We, who entered childhood in the late 1930's, received a healthy, controlled diet, growing up in clean streets enjoying simple homemade pleasures. Today, we eat more than our stomachs can digest and buy all our pleasures and then throw them away.

We are travelling faster than our guardian angels can fly. We are ghosting our towns as we shop in our chairs. Our police are armed soldiers; our soldiers are peacekeepers.

We no longer sing; we shout and scream. We no longer talk; we no longer walk. We talk with our fingers, our heads bending low as we go on our way in silent communication.

We are splitting our nation and weakening our strength. We fiddle, like Nero, as the world falls apart. We are slow to respond to the speed of change.

The changes in my lifetime are only the start. We are handing ourselves over to robotic technology and artificial intelligence. Will young life be found for sale on supermarket shelves and procreation of life by BOGOF?

Am I right to be worried as my days come to an end? Did my grandparents think likewise as worship declined? Will children know where beetroot comes from or laugh and play in clean water and clean air?

Fear not, say my children. We can travel the globe and see each other with the touch of a screen. We live in, and embrace, a diverse multicultural world. Our homes are heated; our health is protected. Relax, technology will prevail and save the earth.

That's young optimism, not old pessimism, I guess.

CONTENTS - PART 1

CONTENTS - PART 2

PART 1

Reflective Poems

by an

Old Codger

Image by Ben Tattersall, grandson

THIS TINY ISLAND - 1

This tiny island so scarred and stained
By picks and shovels and muscles strained,
Deep in the bowels of this precious land
Men sweated and ached heaving coal by hand.

Dust in lungs, cuts in hands,
Scars on skin, wet clothes just hang
On bodies bent low swinging at coal,
Dynamite ready to shove in the hole.

Props take the strain with creaking and moan,
Black gold, false gold, rubble and stone
Is shovelled away for onward transmission,
Into small wheeled wagons for human consumption.

Women and children in homemade shawls,
Stagger against winds up to the mills,
Wide leather belts slide overhead,
Very long hours for pieces of bread.

Health is a threat, dust is the curse,
Accidents happen, there is no nurse.
It's not safe for children, it's not safe for girls,
A slip of the belt and off go their curls.

Technology came and workers sat down
In front of a switch, a lever, in gowns
And hairnets, gloves, glasses
And protection from sounds.

Then skills were replaced by robots and things
That never get tired and don't even sing.
They never complain, they never get stiff,
They never sit down in a Union tiff.

The workers sit down but now in a chair,
By their fire or TV with an air of despair.
Freedom from toil, freedom from sweat
But missing their pals, and not feeling great.

This tiny island so scarred and stained,
Reflects the past, the young must be trained
To recover the land and sea and the air we breathe.
Sadly, this land to them we now bequeath.

THIS TINY ISLAND – 2

Mary has a little lamb,
Its fleece worth less than a jar of jam.
Woollen mills are long forgotten,
It's polyester now or Chinese cotton.

Harry has a herd of cattle
But badgers really make him rattle.
Call the vet to check their necks,
Take a chair and write the cheques.

Tom has a flock of laying fowl
But he may have to throw in the towel.
He needs to check his biosecurity,
To lose his birds would be a great pity.

A farmer's job is full of strife,
As herdsmen no longer like the life.
Indoor farming or open-air?
Is the future meat or flour?

Market prices up and down,
Trade barriers and documentation,
Land, water and air pollution,
But technology may be the solution.

Four by Fours and quad bikes too,
Replace lost labour, now so few.
One giant combine does the job,
But it costs a jolly few "bob".

Many small farms swallowed up
Into ranches, will it stop?
Salvation rests on the scale of operation
And not forgetting diversification.

But when things are tough
And one thinks 'enough',
One loyal friend is always there,
Four legs, a tail, and an eager stare.

THIS TINY ISLAND – 3

In years gone by
Before man could fly,
Unmade lanes and bridle ways
Let man and beast go on their way.

Dust on clothing and on chest,
Watering holes and Inns to rest.
Pace was slow and fraught with fear,
Time stood still for many a year.

Then iron tracks and harnessed steam,
Cobbled roads and boats of narrow beam,
Moved man and goods around the land,
Technology had arrived to give a helping hand.

Then two strokes, four strokes, pneumatic tyres,
Flick a switch and the engine fires.
Wider roads and tarmacadam,
Encouraged speed and many a jam.

Petrol, diesel all from oil
Polluting air, and sea, and soil.
Wider, longer cars to buy,
Faster than our Guardian Angel can fly.

SUVs, MPVs, AEB and Cruise Control,
Sliding doors, Crossover things and Hybrids roll,
Our tiny island is under strain,
With overcrowded roads and trains.

Forget the car for urban travel,
Technology will soon unravel,
Flying taxis, and city airbus in the sky,
Your VTOL pickup will be standing nearby!

(VTOL – Vertical Take Off and Landing)

REFLECTIONS ON LIFE

There was a time not long ago,
When life's pace was rather slow,
Thrift was the key to survive
Patience was the essence of life.

Instant food came from a tin
Or from street vans with hot or cold bins,
Fried fish and chips with mushy peas,
Fresh cod caught from our own closed seas.

Instant pudding was quickly fixed,
Ice cream in cornets or between two biscuits.
Lick it quick or you would regret it,
All that paid for with a thrupenny bit.

That unhealthy diet persists still
And now results in medicine and pill,
Threatening short life for many a citizen
And high costs for our health services across the nation.

War-time rations ensured healthy food,
Experts created meals that were nutritious and good.
All controlled by books of coupons,
No luxuries, cosmetics, or scintillating nylons

Public transport was there for all, not the few,
Buses ran on time and with two crew.
Driver and conductor kept us safe and sound,
You could travel miles for just a pound.

A team of inspectors, very astute,
Awaited buses at points en-route,
Checking if all had paid their fares,
As they moved around and up the stairs.

Similar crews were employed on trains,
Where comfort and ride eased backs and pains.
Carriages were designed with lots of plush seats,
In brocade and with antimacassars, oh so sweet!

Whilst public houses closed their doors at ten
And dancing stopped at the twelve strokes of Big Ben.
All went home and left peaceful streets,
Helping the Bobbies on their beats.

Private cars were for the few and not the many,
For Fords or Austins cost a lot more than a penny.
AA and RAC motorcyclists came into play
Saluting each car, their badge on display.

Respect was shown for man and tools,
Knives and axes were not for fools.
Enoch Powell warned us of his fears,
Streets would flow with blood and tears.

Cinemagoers stood for our National Anthem,
The young stood and the elderly thanked them
On full buses and trains, as they hung on to the straps
And we said 'Hello' and we tipped our caps.

Alas, we have no time to stand and stare,
Talk face to face or offer care,
We are seeking instant gratification,
And losing the soul of our dear nation.

THE FAIR'S IN TOWN

Seaside Fairs are always there,
Offering rides and tunnels to scare.
Travelling Fairs give equal thrill,
Quickly assembled by men with skill.

The Fair's in town,
The word goes around,
Can I have just half a crown?
So I can ride round and round.

Bus to town in expectation,
I hear the noise with great elation,
Bright lights, screams and music too,
I hope that I don't have to queue.

The weekly market space has changed,
A corral of vans has been arranged
With generators running to power each ride
And cables stretching far and wide

The Fairground rides both big and small,
Painted in kaleidoscopic colours all,
Swing or spin in dazzling light
Oh! It is a wonderful sight.

Front of stage as I arrive,
The Waltzer stands to greet, I am alive,

The Big Wheel atop the lot
It's been given the central spot.

The Dodgems with their electric poles,
Driven by some uncertain souls
Trying to ride around keeping clear,
But bumped at front and bumped at rear.

The Wall of Death is worth a call,
As two motorcyclists ride around the cylindrical wall,
Up and down the sides at fullest throttle,
They really must have a lot of bottle.

Colourful horses with wild eyes and nostrils flaring,
Bucking you up and down, but it isn't scaring
On the Carousel of pure delight,
Oh! It is a marvellous sight.

The Rotor Drum attracts us all,
Stand on the floor, back to the wall,
Slow to start, the drum spins round
Faster and faster, there is no sound.

Riders are pinned back and cannot move
As the floor drops away, a law to prove,
Centrifugal force has come into play,
Against the wall the riders stay!

A line of stalls border one side,
To test your skills or hurt your pride.
Roll a penny on to a numbered square,
'It's on the line'. Oh! That's not fair.

Shooting gallery with rifle and target,
Never sure if the sights are perfect,
And Coconut Shies a great temptation,
But are they loose or 'tight' on their station?

Behind the curtain sits the Bearded Lady,
But that all sounds a little shady.
Take a challenge and fight their boxer,
Stay upright until he "Socks Yer".

Have I missed any ride or stall?
Somewhat deaf but enjoyed them all,
Up in the air or spinning around
I have spent my half a crown.

It's been magic time in my old town,
The Fair has just not let me down.
It's time to leave with just a tear,
But they'll be back again next year.

THE TAID I NEVER KNEW

Miner John Robert Jones of Ffynnongroyw,
Made a move we all since rue.
He took my Nain and children too,
To the Welsh east border where coal seams grew.

He settled above the Alyn valley so steep,
To hew out coal two thousand feet deep,
At Gresford colliery across the green valley
Where near two thousand men had an underground tally.

They came from villages old and new,
For other jobs were rare and few.
The Dennis shaft took fresh air down for men to suck
As each one filled a two wheeled truck.

My mother learnt from Taid of their unbearable state,
They knew the risks and their possible fate.
Machinery noise and dust and fumes,
The growing smell of death that would consume.

This pit so hot they sweated in thin pants or less,
Or worked waist high in water of a dirty mess.
They strained their eyes in the dust and dark,
Their conditions were brutal and quite stark.

The ultimate happened on a Saturday morning,
At two o'clock, flames swept through so alarming,
Two Hundred and Sixty-Two met their death,
They didn't even have time to catch their breath.

Too many men were working that Dennis patch,
As some had swapped their day shift, to watch
The Carnival and 'Derby Match' in town that day.
We should remember all their souls and pray.

Three of the Rescue Team were killed by gas,
And one surface worker died by an unexpected blas
The final toll was Two Hundred and Sixty-Six souls,
Needless deaths as the village church bell tolls.

That torrid day the land stood still, as death hovers
Over wives and mothers, friends, and brothers,
Sons and daughters and many more
Frozen in shock, despair and sore.

The pit was sealed, evidence that none had survived,
No bodies to bury, just memories of when they lived.
Funds raised, tributes paid; questions and inquires made.
We cannot let the sacrifice by those honest miners' fade.

The skylarks sang that Saturday morn,
High above the valley and fields of corn.
I heard those larks sing as there I grew
Over the grave of the Taid I never knew.

WE MUST REMEMBER

"Gone to start the Wine Committee"
So runs this shortened ditty,
On a headstone plain and grey,
In a field so quiet where you can pray.

The friends that this soul left behind
Have placed this stone, so kind,
High on the hillside for some reflection,
In memory of a man they held with affection.

He had strayed across the Irish Sea
From his homeland and his family,
To live a life and settle down
In an old welsh castle town.

Across the Channel at Normandy
In peaceful maintained cemeteries,
Thousands of colleagues buried in sorrow,
Who gave their young lives for our tomorrow.

All are heroes no matter their rank,
For our peace we have them to thank.
They too lie far from home, at rest,
Simple graves in lines abreast.

We may not know from where they came,
Or how they fought and then were slain.
But *"Memory is a golden chain*
To bind us till we meet again."

DISTANT CHILDHOOD MEMORIES

As I sit and ponder what's in store,
My thoughts go back more and more,
To childhood times when life was simple,
We knew no other and what food was ample.

Wars were raging East and West,
Miners and steelworkers doing their best,
Output was high to meet the demand,
I guess those chaps were feeling grand.

Lying in bed in the still of the evening,
Miners below cutting coal by machining,
Vibrating sounds came up to my bed,
I felt connected, it has to be said.

Each night I had another treat,
Miners' boots clip clopping on the street
As they came home from their shift,
Or leaving to drop down in the lift.

I lived on the edge of a valley incline,
On the far side ran the Great Western line.
Chester to Wrexham and on, as you go,
Passenger service and goods, to and fro.

At the brow of the valley across the way,
Gresford church tower stood tall and grey,
Its bells one of the seven wonders of Wales
Pealing out across the valley it regales.

Lying in bed on a damp Autumn night,
The sound of a goods train out of sight,
Chug, chug, chugging crossing the border,
Approaching my valley, its' sound getting stronger.

Ahead lies the Gresford incline that needs a good pull,
More steam for the boiler, the waggons are full.
The engine is straining but the wheels lose their grip,
The whole train is starting to slip!

The loud sound now is a shuddering noise
Until silence, with brakes on, the whole in a poise.
Quietness over the valley for quite a while,
Waiting for the cavalry to arrive from many a mile.

Finally, in the far distance the sound of help,
An engine is coming at quite a belt.
It toots its presence, acknowledgement signed,
A pull from the front, a push from behind.

Finally, silence is back, the train on its way,
I lie back, it will all happen again on another day.
One other memory that tickled me,
Was each Christmas day on the BBC.

With latest technology to please the nation,
The Beeb always transmitted a Christmas celebration
With sounds from across the nation,
And Gresford church bells were on its station.

I found it fascinating to stand at the back door
Hearing the bells on the radio
And coming across the valley, both in sync,
It really did tickle me pink.

As Karen Carpenter often sung,
We listened to the radio when we were young.
"Dick Barton-Special Agent" and ITMA comedy,
Workers Playtime and Radio Caroline out at sea.

Simple things like cinema spool films,
Hollywood cowboys and Cherokee Indians,
Laurel and Hardy, Old Mother Riley,
Sounds and songs and black and white films to see.

Whist I was enjoying my young childhood life,
Making catapults, bows and arrows, with my
tortoiseshell knife,
Providing boyhood weapons for fantasy playing,
Real ordnance was being used for maiming and slaying.

Those two worlds in parallel, reflect
A world today that we have to reject.
Violence and genocide on a scale way off the ceiling,
World Leaders playing verbal games with no feeling.

CAREERS ADVICE – 1950's

In the 1950's when I was a scholar,
Blazer and flannels, tie, and clean collar,
Eight years after the end of hostilities
It was recovery, repair and things called utilities.

Ignorance of life in all its forms and fobs,
Unfamiliarity with prospects, direction, jobs,
And careers advice was not forthcoming,
Just follow your dad, at the end of your schooling.

Plodding on through each school year,
Rote learning, impersonal, not endearing.
Our home facilities were often slight,
For books and journals, space, and light.

Our final year had just begun,
Estimates needed on number staying on.
They called it Careers Interview, but it cut no ice
As we stood in line outside the Headmaster's office.

One by one, we were called into his room,
Head and deputy sat ensconced in their visual gloom.
Two elderly welsh men, one stout, one thin,
I stood waiting for one to begin.

'What do you want to do?' the headmaster said,
The other gent sat nodding his head.
'Draughtsmanship' I replied, as if I knew,
One turned grey, the other looked askew.
'Humph' said the Head, looking down in despair,
And I could see that he hadn't much hair.
That was the end of my career interview,
Directed back to my class and my pew.

Those two welsh gentlemen of academic thinking
Knew only of teaching and preaching,
And perhaps a little of male voice singing,
But not what skills our land was needing.

We carved our own destiny with a lot of pluck,
No guidance, no steer, it was a matter of luck.
We grew up fast, worked long hours,
Just two percent went up to Universities' ancient towers.

Just twenty-two Universities then, for the two percent.
Today, one hundred and thirty accepting fifty percent.
Courses across all spectrums of leisure and working life,
Some with intensive content, hard study, no party life.

Others better suited to 'On- the- job' learning,
Where they could be trained and enjoy earning.
No fees were paid in those austere post-war years,
Now graduates have fees to pay, with possible tears.

It's good to have a focused dream
But things aren't always as they seem.
I knew a lad who left his options all behind,
But his childhood dream died, he was colour blind.

"A man that looks on glass,
On it may stay his eye;
Or, if he pleases, through it pass,
And then the heavens espy."   A&M 337 vv2

WAR and BONDING

I was born during a very hot August Bank Holiday time
At two after Noon, and so Leo is my sign,
At my Grandmother's home, a widow of tears,
In a mining village of just some teenage years.

A Coronation year, 999 calls and Sellotape so sticky,
And the year of the Dandy comic weekly,
With Desperate Dan, the world's strongest man
Who could lift a cow with just one hand.

The year of Snow White, the animated film,
And future stars Charlton, Banks, Joan Collins, so slim,
Hopkins, Courtenay, Vanessa Redgrave and Cook,
Who later, no doubt, would each write a book.

A miner's daughter and a miner's son
Created this little bundle of fun,
At ten pounds weight and first-born child,
I guess they both went crazy and a little wild!

A house to rent, just take your pick,
Choice of three built in Ruabon Brick
Had been offered and one they chose,
A couple of years back when they took their vows.

That year the Hindenburg airship went up in fire
And worrying signs nearer home looked dire,
As Britain tried to mediate but had no clout
And two years later a dreadful war broke out.

After my second birthday, of which I have no account,
Chamberlain announced that war had broken out.
Blackout of all lights, Home Guard, and rationing began,
Coupon books from the Ministry of Food met the plan.

Shortages began to bite; Petrol in the Autumn of '39,
But horse and cart for our milk and coal held the line.
And those fine Shires offered a welcome extra home aid,
Gardeners were quick out with their bucket and spade.

Then came bacon, butter, and sugar, each a small square,
Removed from the book, cupboards now quite bare.
September '53 when sugar rationing came to an end
The summer of '54 for the rest of food that was rationed.

Our Regular troops went to France to fight,
Only to lose the game and had to take flight.
Reservists were called into action to stop another retreat
And my father left home for service in the Far East.

When I was two with a head full of curls
And milk teeth shining like a row of pearls,
Men with sons became men with guns
And sons became guardians of their mums.

For many a night my mother and me
Sat by the radio after our tea,
We crept under the stairs when 'Gerry' flew past
To drop bombs on Liverpool with an almighty blast.

I went to school and church and did my bit,
Ran errands to shops with my bowler and stick.
Made bows and arrows, catapults, and kites,
Barrage Balloons tethered over industrial sites.

I was eight years of age when both wars ceased
And a man, called father, came home from the East.
He walked down the street having got off the bus,
The folk all around him making a fuss.

I watched with my pals from across the street,
As he kissed my dear mother, it was quite so sweet.
They both went inside, now what do I do?
Did he see me, did he know me, I hadn't a clue.

So this was the guy who clashed with the Japs,
Travelled back home with all the brave chaps.
My father's come home and out of all danger,
But how does a boy now bond with a stranger?

TROUSERS

My wife keeps on reminding me
That nine men die every year.
Is it too much greed or too much sup?
No, it's putting their trousers on standing up.

The matter of trousers is one you see
That brings the Victor Meldrew out in me,
With slim fit, now today's drainpipe,
Tailored fit, regular fit and all the hype.

The inside leg that's not my size,
A 'comfort waist' that will never win a prize,
Only in the fashion world for a younger guy.
Oh! Its real comfort that I seek to buy.

Chinos with four-inch zips offer inadequate flies,
Hipsters, flat front, pleat front, full kick tape and ties.
Cotton or wool, cord or moleskin, lycra or elastane,
Buying trousers is driving me insane.

Is it me or are there others?
Who miss the staff, acting like personal brothers
In Gents Outfitters, with first-class service of long ago?
Alas, one-stop shopping has seen them go.

I cannot wear trousers like Charlie Chaplin,
Many do on our streets today, it's quite a laugh-in.
Or tight "designer wear" with a rip and a tear,
That would just allow me to sit in my rocking chair.

What is the answer to my plight?
Wear shorts and just go out at night.
I've suffered this problem right up to the hilt,
I know! I'll join the Scots and wear a kilt!

TECHNOLOGY and PACE OF CHANGE

Where I was born and lived in during my boyhood age
Early motoring maps called it the 'Model Village'.
The colliery provided every home with electricity,
Which met the demands of households' every amenity.

In the '30s and 40's with austere times across our land,
Radio sets, street and home lights were the only demand.
Large locked distribution stations located strategically,
With smaller sub-stations placed within our community.

Across my street, in the front garden alongside flowers
and small trees,
Stood one such station, humming away merrily along
with the bees.
Un-noticed, un-loved, but things would change as life
got better,
The mines were nationalised, and miners pay was
greater.

TVs were rented, hoovers and irons, cookers, fridges
and sewing machinery,
Electrical goods were in our shops, the start of retail
therapy.
The load too great for the village's electricity supply
down the line,
Our substation glowed in the dark, the smoke and flames
were quite sublime.

Out went our lights, TV and kettle, on many an occasion,
We then had to sit and wait for the pit electrician.
But here was the rub; Ted had a moonlighting job first,
He was also the village cinema projectionist.

No chance of light or a cup of tea until way past ten,
When Ted would mount his bicycle with torch and then
Cycle down the village to attend to the burnt out 'den'.
Mum and Dad so tolerant, happening again and again.

Things had to change, technology was moving at a pace
My self-contained village, a true model, had been an ace.
Electricity provision nationalised into Electricity Boards,
Village rewired, removing our mercury-filled boards!!

As today's newspaper is tomorrow's chip wrapping,
Today's technology is tomorrow's recycling.
Those mercury switches were akin to asbestos dust,
We learn, we develop, but with a great deal of trust.

IF ONLY I HAD ASKED

An old lipstick of magenta red,
A powder puff somewhat shred,
An old leather glove all alone,
A hairgrip and a tooth-short comb.

A child's drawing, a lace handkerchief,
A cupboard key, a flattened leaf,
A couple of mints, an old bus ticket,
A leaking pen and a stale old biscuit.

A fading photo of my old dad,
Cheeky smile, he looks a cad,
A couple of coins of pre-decimal day,
A Christmas postage stamp in decay.

This pleated handbag with short leather strap,
A brass clasp that shuts with a crispy 'snap'
Holds tokens of life well spent
And a safe for keeping the weekly rent.

This old handbag has seen some life,
Many a pleasure and no doubt strife.
If each could talk and tell its tale,
Her life, her loves, we would unveil.

I never asked our dear old mum
Of what she did when she was young,
Who she met and where she went?
I should have asked, now I'll repent.

So, find the time to quiz us old ones
Before we become just skin and bones.
Life's too short and memories fade,
All your efforts will be repaid.

WHY?

Why do lady hairdressers wear black?
Is it in memory of the hair they hack?
Why do butchers wear striped aprons?
As they cut red meat off the bones.

Why do bakers wear white clothes?
As they bake their bread and scones.
Why do vicars wear white collars at the neck?
And Scotsmen dance in plaid and check?

Why do soldiers all dress the same?
Fighting evil who don't play the game
And dress like anyone in the street,
Hoping that they will not be beat?

Why do rugby players wear coloured shirts?
When they all end up covered in dirt.
Why do policemen wear dark blue?
Better still in a coloured hue.

Why do judges wear gowns and wigs?
And the Jews cannot eat any pigs.
Why are nurses dressed in blue?
Oh, they are so caring and so true.

Why don't ships sink when on the ocean?
When submarines sink deep with sliding motion.
How do aeroplanes fly so high?
Are they touching the stars in the sky?

These small thoughts are noted here,
For those stressed fathers with children dear,
Who with their young enquiring minds,
Will ask such questions and similar kinds.

So be prepared and think of more,
I'm off, I have a malt to pour.

STEP CHANGES

A German company came to see
If coal was lying beneath this lea.
The land was flat up to the valley top
With coal mines around, quite a crop.

Some pilot holes were drilled down to a level,
Samples taken, the news was sound and well.
Then work just stopped, the men retracted,
World War 1 broke put and progress halted.

Peacetime came and the men came back,
A shaft was bored, the earth turned black.
Nissan huts housed miners who excavated
Whilst a 'model' village could be created.

Half the stock built by the mining company,
The other half by the local council authority.
The mindset and level of the latter's technology
Reveals their step change in housing strategy.

Toilets that were down in the garden, take a torch,
Now moved within the backdoor porch.
Indoor flush but beware a caller to the back door,
Now you are trapped, offering up a natural odour.

Old stock was heated by town gas or coal,
No upper heat or light for any poor soul.
Coal delivered to shed, or cellar, or at the gate,
Bucketed in to fuel the boiler or the grate.

The 'model' village houses had coal delivered
To a coal store located at the back door.
But no piped radiated heat, you just shivered,
Or lit coal fireplaces on ground and upper floor.

Miners came home from a twelve-hour shift
Covered in dry sweat, coal dust, dirt, and grit.
Tin baths with hot water by the kitchen fire
Gave pain relief whilst cleaning every pore and fibre.

Those Council chaps now made another step change,
A plumbed bathroom, en-suite to the kitchen range!
Privacy was not a given for any weekly scrub
And still no plumbed heat around this family hub.

I grew up in this 'model' house for twenty-two years
Many still endured the old life with laughter and tears.
No fitted kitchens with all mod cons to hand,
Just love and kindness and a neighbourhood band.

This brief personal note on social history,
Conveys the small steps of developing technology
That the Western world took time to digest,
To learn, to build, consolidate, and test.

But the Developing nations are jumping those years,
Those formative stages of success and tears,
Those steps of progress over time and learning,
Now thrust forward into a world of constant yearning.

But do all the years of knowledge and experience
Matter when man is being replaced by clever science.
The learning direction is no longer a step change caper
But innovation and a blank sheet of paper.

HOLIDAY TIME

There was a time not long ago
When pace of life was rather slow,
Workers given no holiday pay,
Just days off on each Bank Holiday.

A change is as good as a rest they say,
So, a day trip was on if you could pay,
A charabanc to coast or dale,
Compulsory stop for a jug of ale

For some it was thought quite 'hip'
To book a seat on a mystery trip.
Away for a day, no not where,
Is it here or is it there?

No idea, the driver never gave a clue,
Coat or frock, clog or shoe?
A collection taken for the lucky chap
Paid for his lunch before an afternoon nap.

Enjoyed the day, dodged the rain,
Did not help the arthritic pain.
The cold lunch caused quite a fuss,
Where, oh where, did he park the bus?

All aboard, the stragglers arrive,
Time for the long homeward drive.
Refreshed, relaxed, it's time for a song
In unison or harmony, as we roll along.

Our driver is really quite a sweet
As he drops us off at the end of our street.
Arriving home to stark reality
Looking forward to that cup of tea.

Who wants flights to miles away?
To join strangers in a crowded bay,
Eating chips and things with fancy names,
Indigestion and strange stomach pains

Stay right here, as we had to do
When holidays abroad were for a few.
Don't pollute our air just for fun
Or burn your skin by extreme sun.

Protect the planet, save the earth,
Think of those just achieving birth
Imagine life as the earth expires
Consumed by ash and monstrous fires.

THE PENDULUM SWINGS

In the 1700's, cottage-based work was just small scale,
In houses and farms, for local sale.
Hand crafted items, one at a time, almost a penance,
Slow to create by self-employed tenants.

Urban industrial developments began to grow,
Our population was swelling but production was slow.
Clever inventors made machines that harnessed water
And new products were made faster and faster.

The self-employed who left the countryside
Became paid employees working side by side,
On fast machines that kept on going,
So different from their handmade sewing.

As time moved on and the years rolled by,
Manufacturing goods would metaphorically 'fly'
Out of the factories, carried by water, rail or road
And man's freedom began to erode.

Clock on, clock off, and keep it running,
No time to chat, no time for singing,
Check for errors, check for size,
Factory life and offices too strained the eyes.
Day's work done, but there's no prize,
We had all become industrialised.

But this old factory life has nearly gone,
They are running them now with almost no-one.
And those men of skill now replaced by robots,
Are in allotments left growing peas and shallots.

But here's the thing,
It's the pendulum swing.
The Cottage industry has arrived
Helping man to survive.

Self-employment is the way for many,
Working from home to make a penny
Or two, with technology the saving grace,
We have a newly growing working race.

Our dear old forefathers and mothers
Plied locally their goods to others,
But there is no limit to trading spheres
Enterprising persons should have no fears.

The world wide web has opened every door
Of opportunity and more,
The situations and limitations of long ago
Have gone and you should now get up and go.

'DEMOB' SUITS

Our troops returned home to great acclaim,
From battlefields, airfields, and seas they came,
Home to families, loved ones, young and old,
Having endured heat and sweat, ice and cold.

Some returned with battle scars outside,
Many with memories all locked inside
Of capture, torture, death, mosquitoes, flies,
Shell shock, and bombs dropping from the skies.

Life at the front, in foreign lands and seas,
Rationed food, and bullied beef and peas
Resulted in loss of weight and size and frame,
Wearing clothes left back home was never the same.

Demob suits were freely given of varying sizes,
To spot an ex-trooper there were no prizes.
It was out of one uniform and into another,
Pinstripe, two shirts, tie, shoes, and outer cover.

Seventy-five thousand suits were made each week,
A matter of luck if you had one that didn't need a tweek.
Quality cloth, from Burtons and others, lasted years
For family gatherings of pleasure and of tears.

The aftermath of conflict offers many a challenge
To recover a nation and help it manage
To achieve a peaceful, progressive, life.
There are so many nations today living in strife,

They need more than suits, hats, and ties,
It's demob homes, work, and safe blue skies.
Investment, support, and infrastructure in place
And leaders of integrity, honesty, and good grace.

MY BOYHOOD VILLAGE

My life began in a modern village
Created when rich seams of coal were pillaged
From under a luscious green field site,
To provide our lives with heat and light.

A German company came to see
If coal was lying beneath this lea.
The land was flat up to the valley top
With coal mines around, quite a crop.

Some pilot holes were drilled down to a level,
Samples taken, the news was sound and well.
Then work just stopped, the men retracted,
World War 1 broke put and progress halted.

Peacetime came and the men came back,
A shaft was bored, the earth turned black.
Nissan huts housed miners who excavated
Whilst a 'model' village could be created.

Two shafts were sunk, it was quite a feat,
The drop to base two thousand four hundred feet.
A model village then came into life,
With avenues and shops, and man and his wife.

A church and chapels and a junior school
Were built within by hand and tool.
These larger assets made quite a presence
But the tunnels below created subsidence.

My school and church began to move,
Cracks appeared, glass gauges were set in walls to prove,
Supported by buttresses of wood and brick,
Attached to the outside walls to do the trick.

It was '42 when I started school in the 'fall',
A simple design of classrooms around a central hall.
But disaster had struck, and things were dire,
The hall was rubble, it had been on fire.

The teaching staff were rather old,
We had to do as we were told.
Rote learning was the means of teaching
Tables, more tables and tendency to preaching.

No books to read and no library,
Assemblies no more, not even temporarily.
No canteen for dinner, we had to walk
In line up to 'top school' and dare not talk.

Community life was very strong,
Essential when World War Two came along
And men worked so hard to meet the national goal,
Their skin bore scars, like tattoos, from flying coal.

Barrage Balloons tethered above the mine,
As Gerry flew over from Ireland, following a line
To drop bombs on Liverpool and Merseyside
A stray bomb fell nearby hitting Ted's horse, it died.

Aside the church was an old Nissan hut – a reminder
Of a redundant home for the first pioneering miner.
It served as Church Hall, Scouts and the Mothers Union,
With coke oven heat and nights of good home-made fun.

Beside the church and hut stood the Cinema Hall
And a well-stocked Boys Club for young miners and all.
A full-time club for those on shifts around the clock,
The club and cinema integrated into one large block.

Across, the Remembrance Garden with the fallen named,
Always well-tended and secure for it to remain
A reminder of those village lads who went away,
A single journey and no return to pay.

But the grandest edifice of all,
The Miners Welfare and its fine dance hall,
With a polished sprung floor from wall to wall,
A raised stage and rotating ball to colour us all.

This grand grey building stood not aloof,
Tennis courts, bowling greens, and a welsh slate roof.
Children's playground with excited cries,
Cricket ground, pavilion, bandstand, a sight for the eyes.

The Council stepped in to provide more homes,
The village stock doubled with two village phones.
The houses needed power, the colliery was willing,
The weekly 'light man' called just for a shilling. (5p)

The annual Rose Show reflected the gardening affection
Of miners and others so proud of their collection
Of fruit, veg, and floral displays of blooms and sprays,
That scented the air and our clothes for several days.

The September Carnival day was colourful and gay,
With Carnival Queens from villages near and far away.
Troops of young female Morris Dancers on the field
Throughout the day all hoping to win the coveted shield.

The parade began assembled at the top of the village,
Passed down through all the streets for quite an age.
They finally arrived at the Welfare field of mowed grass,
Dancers, Queens, and those in fantastic fancy dress.

The colliery managers gave full support to these events,
The families enjoyed those days, always well content.
Off home in the setting sun to sleep sound and refreshed,
Village folk appreciating their efforts and felt well blest.

The mine closed in '66 and the village lost its identity,
No common goal, no common aim, no entity,
Families left to find coal elsewhere in a dying trade,
The village tries to follow the past that the colliery made.

A cosmopolitan village has filled the space,
A cleaner place, a bigger place,
Light industries all around have arrived,
I hope my boyhood village will continue to thrive.

1960's and MORE

The 1960's was a pivotal time,
Second age of feminism came on-line.
Hippies, miniskirts and 'burn your bra',
Computer mouse and hatchback car.

Beach Boys, Hendrix, Bardot and Dylan,
Baez, Connery, Hepburn and Streisand.
Space race to the moon watched by all,
Touch-tone phones and the Berlin Wall.

Living in a time of change for all,
Clothes and Hair, Rock and Roll.
Cold war tension with nuclear threat,
Gay rights and bikinis that made men sweat.

Macmillan spoke of 'the wind of change'
It was a wind of both width and range.
Science, fashion, lifestyle, and food,
He also said: 'We've never had it so good'.

In 1963, at the Cinema in the local town,
I witnessed the change in music, its delivery, and sound.
I took a coach full of RAF lads, their evening was free,
I sat in the stalls not sure what to see.

The Top of the Bill was Chris Montez of 'Lets' Dance',
The first half went well, as I sat in a Music Hall trance.
The interval came and I saw all around
The young audience had begun walking up and down.

The safety curtain went up for the second half,
But the youngster kept moving and having a laugh.
Centre stage stood a static Gerry Dorsey* trying to sing,
This audience ignored him, with an atmosphere growing.

Poor chap, he hadn't a chance at all,
Stood thinking "How soon can I leave this Hall".
As he finished his act the tension was rising,
I soon realised why; it wasn't surprising.

On ran four slight lads dressed in dark suits,
With mop top hair, and certainly not brutes.
They say there were four, of similar age,
But I swear I saw five as they covered the stage.

The youngsters yelled as they stood on the piano,
Not stopping, they sang, played, entertaining ever so.
The Hall was alive, a new era was coming into play,
The Beatles were here and here they would stay.

I witnessed first-hand an act like a seer,
That night their message was loud and clear.
No longer static performances at work or play,
It's dynamic action that will always hold sway.

*Gerry Dorsey very soon after this event
became Engelbert Humperdinck
of "I'll never fall in love again."

** See rear book cover

MY MOTHER

"You weren't born rich, lad,
But I think you were born lucky."

And she was right, that's for sure,
My mother's assessment of my future.
I have lived a life both lucky and rich,
Not in money but in life's free gifts.

Born the year our King caught a cold and died.
Dr Crippen poisoned his wife and she died too!
The Boy Scout Association was born for men
And so was my mum, Mair Jones, in nineteen ten.

She left school at thirteen years,
Glad to go, she shed no tears.
Lessons focused on the 3Rs and pliancy,
And chunks of domestic science a necessity.

With golden red hair she endured teasing
By pupils, teachers, and her siblings,
Her native tongue was the banned welsh language,
Disciplined every time she uttered a Cymraeg passage.

My mother went to work as a domestic servant,
Non-stop skivvy, on your knees or leaning bent,
The time of shared cold water tap and dare not laugh,
Dolly tub, outside privy and weekly bath.

Up at dawn and on the go,
Fires lit, tables laid, keep head low.
Life expectancy, if at birth you survive,
Men at fifty-two, women at fifty-five.

Working class girls and women had few choices,
Encouraged to serve others and mind their voices.
Consider the interests of their menfolk was the message,
Second class lifestyle for them, throughout that age.

She didn't last long and came back to her home life,
To help her parents and give support with the strife
Of mining father and brothers seeking employment,
Whilst making music was their enjoyment.

With piano and violin to hand,
They created a popular village band,
Playing for dancing each Saturday night,
'Till radio bands stole their local limelight.

My mother's life was one of caring,
Giving up her newly married dwelling,
Sacrificing stability of a settled life
To answer the call of those in strife.

Widowed uncle-in-law with damp cottage plaster,
Widowed mother, father killed in mining disaster.
Then mother-in-law in failing health and bed-ridden,
Responding to their health and their every bidding.

But my mother had an open face and sweet voice,
Loved to sing those 20's musical songs, her choice
Was Ivor Novello's 'We'll Gather Lilac in the Spring',
'Waltz of My Heart'; with me she often loved to sing.

Like so many others of that time and suppression
Life was tough with little compassion.
She was neither rich nor lucky but had courage
To endure and thankfully live to a ripe old age.

Her later life was kind and full of pleasures,
Thanks to that step change in domestic measures.
Fridges, freezers, hoovers, cookers, phones and TV,
Motor car to take her and hubby on trips to hill and sea.

Son and daughter grown up, married, and doing well,
Grand children giving pleasure, casting their spell,
Time to read and knit and sew for one and all,
Mothers Union meetings in the old church Hall.

One pre-Christmas time party at the church hall,
she celebrated
With her village friends, good fun, no chance of being
inebriated,
Walked back home and settled down, but life took a turn
that night,
Her life decayed and she died, but her star above
is shining bright.

MY GARDEN IN THE RAIN

As I watch through the windowpane,
The Heavens open and release the rain.
I'm grateful for this summer burst,
It must surely quench the earth's outstanding thirst.

The dark grey clouds are slowly moving by,
I've lost the sun shining in the sky.
Holly leaves glisten as the rain comes down,
Washing away the summer dust of fine light brown.

The global heads in my dahlia beds
Look sodden as they slowly lower their heads,
Stalks of the cones of my Paniculata bush
Bend over in an arc of beaten hush.

Alas, my rosebuds may not survive
And bloom to their full beauty and thrive,
But just turn brown and hang in shame
As they lie sodden and give up the game.

The pelargoniums just love the sun
To sit in damp pots will be no fun,
My early cuttings will save the day,
I'll have new plants and not have to pay.

Leaves of my potatoes have been a healthy sight
But this damp weather will encourage blight.
A watching brief must now entail,
Or my promised crop will surely fail.

The lawn refreshed by the steady fall,
Turns green and strong for any bat and ball.
The lawn is recovering with remarkable speed,
Soon I shall have to spread its Autumn feed.

As I look around at the falling rain,
It isn't all gloom and pain.
Drops of rain like shining beads
Of glass or pearl will swell my summer seeds.

Since life in all its forms began to flow,
Cultivation began a long-time ago,
Come rain or snow, sun and heat,
A garden will always be a perfect retreat.

Early Military Life 1.

OVERALLS, SUIT and TIE, UNIFORM,

IN ONE YEAR

Apprenticeship over, College work done,
Overalls off, polished shoes and office suit on,
Production Engineer now, albeit junior,
Mr Rothwell was our most senior.

A letter arrived from one of those Government bodies,
They were aware I had finished my studies.
I'm now on standby, to be called up for national duty,
So, two years out of my suit and out of Blighty.

Not so, thought I, as an advert I had spied,
"Technical knowhow? It's what we need" it cried,
"Commissions on offer to the right chaps,
So, apply and you are in - if there's no mishaps."
(Or words to that effect!).

Instructions arrived with helpful rail travel,
Off to RAF Biggin Hill's Selection Panel.
Bleak, cold airfield initiatives, one November dawn,
Classroom tests, medical checks down in London Town.

Amongst the Christmas mail on that Christmas Eve,
A letter to report to RAF Jurby, on Epiphany.
Handed in my notice and said my farewells to all,
And a special one to Joy, the girl I loved and cannot call.

Walked down the valley to the railway Halt for the train,
My father came with me, my cases were quite a strain.
Liverpool dock, Isle of Man ferry on a winter's morn,
Sat deep in the decks in case of any unpleasant storm.

The Isle of Man in summer I know is a delight and fun,
Bleak mid-winter, trees grow sideways, there is no sun.
I've left my job, it's tough going and I'll have no rest,
But I'll just keep smiling and try and do my best.

Allocated hut and bed, standard uniform, and beret,
It will be a while before I depart back on the ferry.
Introduced to Mess life, Mess bills, and the protocol,
'Government Property' on every sheet of toilet roll!

We were a motley group in Green Squadron
of four flights,
Older guys and NCOs, university chaps and
some heading for great heights.
Light relief on Sundays as invited organist
for the camp church,
Enjoyed a game of hockey but ended up with a black eye
and a little besmirched.

I was taught to shoot, rapid and single shot,
Into the gas chamber and out again, I was quite hot,
Parade training and regimental skill,
Now quite fit but not expected to kill!

New to me but not for those already in blue,
Welfare, Law, Admin & Org, quite a lot to chew.
Mock interview that stretched me with the patter,
"Elsie Spanner from Ramsey" - a paternity matter.

I became friendly with John, a married ex-maritime guy.
When parcels of cakes arrived from home, by and by,
We feasted on the cakes made by Joy – she's a dream.
'Marry that girl' advised John, as we munched away
through sponge and cream.

We all gathered to hear our fate at the end of Lent,
Were all my efforts, discomfort and time well spent?
I was through but two mates not up to standard,
Directed back home, their National Service had ended!!

Passing out parade went well, the weather was fair,
I was delighted my parents, sister, and fiancé were there.
Back on the ferry, pleasant company and some elation,
Easter leave and off to the RAF School of Education.

Early Military Life 2

BEWARE PRIDE

RAF Uxbridge, home of the RAF School of Education,
Also, the Queen's Flight for any ceremonial occasion,
Tall, smart, lads drilled to perfection,
Excellent example of the standard for any inspection.

We honed our teaching skills on them without protests,
Preparing them all to sit their RAF education tests.
Visual aids, Gestetner and Banda with inky hands,
And well laid out teaching plans.

A pin-suited officer up from the 'Smoke',
Came to discuss postings, of which we then spoke.
"I'm posting you to No 4 School of Technical Training
To teach Engineering Drawing and enhance
the boys' learning."

Arrived, and duly reported to a Squadron Leader,
"Sir, posted in as instructed and I have my gear."
This old chap, a dour Scot, leaned back in his chair,
Frustrated expression, a look of distain and despair.

"What the hell is going on down in the Air Ministry,
We stopped teaching that subject – that's now history.
You're teaching Maths, Science and Radio technology,
Two weeks to prepare for the start of the next Entry."

Two thousand Boy Entrants learning various trades,
All seeking success and the highest of grades,
Moving from boyhood into manhood and maturity,
Pay parades on Thursdays, Church Parades obligatory.

As the weeks went on and the topics taught in silence,
Resistance, Capacitance and relevant laws of science,
Transmission, Reception and valve radio construction,
My confidence building beyond my expectation.

The lads mistook my presentation and tuition,
As someone who could repair a faulty radio station.
I had not noticed as I entered the class place,
One young lad brought with him a 'weekend' case.

As they sat in awe at my knowledge and explanation,
A hand went up, could I recover his radio station?
At that point, I dropped a fundamental clanger,
My response should have been to 'see me later.'

"Let me have a look," I spoke like an Ace.
Up came the lad with his radio suitcase,
"I lose the station when I turn this switch knob".
I opened the back with a coin worth a 'bob'.

Tentatively, peering down into a complex box of tricks,
The battery within was the size of household bricks.
Wires were tugged, valves seats given a gentle blow,
Tension rising as the class looked on,
but I really did not know!

Then, what luck, I spotted my salvation,
The knob's spindle circlip, with elation,
Lying at the bottom in all the dust,
Reaching that clip, nothing disturbed, is a must!

With unknown delicacy, the clip extracted,
Fitting it back on the groove was quite protracted.
"There you are lad" I said with pride,
And the class looked on in awe with eyes quite wide.

The following week, the class at work in front of me,
I was prompted to ask the fateful enquiry,
"How's your radio now?" expecting satisfaction to purr,
"It was fine on Friday, blew up on Saturday, Sir!".

That lesson has stayed with me and I am no sage,
But watch your ego, know your limit, stay on message.
Pride comes before the fall,
Write that on your office wall

Early Military Life 3.

A CHALLENGING DECISION

*O*fficers to attend a meeting'; we gathered in uniform
with our hats,
It was 1963, at a time during the Cold War
superpowers' spats.
Tension all around as mutual atomic annihilation
was a possibility,
Just before the Nuclear Test Ban Treaty eased
the hostility.

The Regiment Officer, addressing the gathering
without hesitation
Explained our proximity and vulnerability to the
Midlands conurbation,
That could be a target for a nuclear bomb,
creating huge mortality,
And we must be ready for such an eventuality.

We learned the facts of carnage by a
Russian Nuke blow,
Exploded either in the air, on the ground,
or down below.
The Padre rose to his feet, objected strongly,
and left the room,
The rest of us sat there in an air of gloom.

A practice exercise was due to take place,
Our instructions were given, there would be a race
To head for the airfield and the hangers, grass topped,
Through the gate at which we would be stopped.

There we would receive a note – just for the trial,
We would be given a pistol and a cyanide phial.
The pistol for control of any surging, panicking public,
Cyanide for personal use, the situation quite "Myopic".

A futile solution to the outcome of a dreadful calamity,
Air and water radioactively poisoned,
ground zero just a huge dust cavity.

Communications lost and fallout on the winds
would have sailed
Across the land for miles, thank goodness
that good sense prevailed.

This scenario put me under significant stress,
How would I act at such a time, I must confess?
Would I turn right to the airfield, seeking shelter and life,
Or left, down the lane to be with baby and wife?

Early Military Life 4

NEVER PANIC

I decided to request moving from short-term
to permanent commission,
So sought the signature of my Squadron Leader,
who was on a mission
Seeking a 'volunteer' to attend a Flight Commander's
Recreational course,
Hill walking, rock climbing, abseiling, canoeing
and all things worse.

A deal was struck, off up the hills, my form in the post!
The School of P E, at RAF St Athan, was my initial host.
Canoeing in the pool, skirt tight, thighs against the sides,
Upside down, self-extraction required, and no-one dies.

Then off we went with 'Compo' food boxes and tents,
Up the hills and rocks of Wales, spade for natural events.
My curry powder added taste to every bland meal,
Fresh air and fine scenery, I guess I had a good deal!

Every year, each entry of boys went to summer camp,
A warm-up exercise held first up on the Wrekin 'bank'.
Then on to Wales, high above old Aberystwyth town,
Five day 'legs' to hike and camp, no time to lie down.

My class entry's turn, so I went along as roving monitor,
With colleague Flt.Sgt. Casey, a fine, keen walker.
The boy's Leader decided camping was not for him,
So, I took over, as he left Wales on an unexpected whim!

The weather turned one day, heavy fog and quite damp,
All but one team arrived safely at the appointed camp.
So, Flt/Sgt Casey and I went back on the route in search,
Thick fog and silence all around like an empty church.

Through the gloom, voices somewhere around or ahead,
Anxious voices, the team were lost, it must be said.
We called out loud and clear into the swirling murk,
Voices changed, relief was clear, faces held no smirk.

When life's a fog and your way is lost,
Stay calm, don't panic at any cost.
Help will always be there to offer a hand
And guide you through to your promised land.

Early Military Life 5

SERVICE LIFE

Pay Parade

E very Thursday, at the end of the day,
Parades were held to give the boys their weekly pay,
The amount paid out was part of their remuneration
For serving the Queen and all our nation.
The rest was saved, not for a rainy day,
But for their well-earned leave away.

They lined up alphabetically, at ease,
Two officers at a table ready to please.
One paid out notes, the other the cash,
Then off to the NAAFI I guess they would dash.

Many occasions, when on duty at this parade
I was joined by Dave, my National Service comrade.
Married, his pay was less than that paid out to each lad,
His comments are not for print, but he was mad.

Sports Days

M y Section Leader, in charge of the boy's swimming,
Needed judges, so asked me if I would be willing
To help with the annual swimming gala event.
I explained that such a competition was not my bent.

'You can help by watching the boys in the diving event
And mark their dive down as they hit the pool hell bent,
A smooth entry with no ripples or splash, award a ten,
It was like Strictly Come Diving with a budding Len.

The annual sports day was another affair.
My squadron was short of volunteers, and in despair
I agreed to fill the slot for the one-mile run,
But at the line, stood runners not there for the fun.

Dressed in white gear of superior design,
While I wore my issue blue shorts, too late to resign.
Spiked running shoes and muscles all a 'gleam,
They set off at a pace, I followed in their slip stream.
p.s. I didn't come last.

Four years at this school came to a close,
No better young men I could have chose
To teach, as each entry came, learned, and left
To front-line action, ensuring we would never be bereft.

A signal arrived, I'm on my way, it's not a dream,
To join Trenchard's established Apprenticeship scheme,
At No 1 School of Technical Training in Bucks county.
Teaching thermodynamics and engine technology!

I quickly learned that life is a challenge and never dull,
No task is too challenging, no job too small.
My career in the military would continue to unveil,
All things are possible, take a deep breath,
You will not fail.

Military Life 6.
A GOLDEN RULE

A quick refresh of my old college studies
I'm now at the school that opened in the 1920s.
Lord Trenchard's foresight on work-based learning,
Recruit high quality men and provide internal training.

The School stands on past Rothchild land.
The family manor within the grounds is very grand.
Now the Officers Mess, a place for food, rest, and chats.
I drew back my room curtains and out flew bats!

The academic building houses two large lecture halls,
Main access off the central corridor wide and tall.
Opposite, the Thermodynamics laboratory to support
The classroom teaching, noting data on which to report.

Vehicle engines and research units all bedded down,
Measuring gauges, dynamometers all attached around.
The course moved on to aircraft engine technology,
Compressors, turbines, combustion, and their synchrony.

The Rover car company of some fame had a dream,
'Why not install a jet engine' said one of its racing team.
JET 1 lies in the London Science museum, entry free,
One engine was installed on a rig for our students to see.

The exhaust pipe passed through a hole in the wall,
The noise, when running, would be heard by all,
The gas released freely into the central courtyard.
Ear defenders on, so discussion with students was hard.

I would take members of the class down below
To the lab, to take readings of pressure and fuel flow.
A retired service man was the laboratory technician,
He would fuel up and make ready for the ignition.

I started the jet, the lads with note pads around the bay,
Suddenly, control was lost, the jet was racing away.
The lads bolted off to the corridor out through the door,
The technician ran away and took shelter in his store.

I stood alone, the jet engine screaming,
My thoughts were racing, I wasn't dreaming,
I had to stop this monster before it 'flew',
The answer was clear, cut off the fuel, turn the screw.

Years before, during my apprenticeship days,
I spent many hours on machine shop lathes,
One valuable piece of advice I took to heart,
Know how to stop before you begin to start.

The lecture halls rose up to the higher floor,
I often gazed at the seating to the upper door
Where hundreds had sat and went off to war and strife.
Some gained high rank but many, sadly, gave their life.

The curse of wars that have broken many a heart
Is not knowing how to stop before they start.
The world would be rid of man-made sin
If Leaders remembered this and wars would not begin.

AN ASYMMETRICAL LOW BRIDGE BUS

Sitting on the lower deck right hand seats
Of a 50's double decker bus, reads a sign so neat
'Lower your head when leaving your seat'.

You're sitting on an AEC 'Low bridge' bus,
If you stood up tall there would be such a fuss,
A sore head, a broken neck, days in bed,
There's a sunken ceiling above your head.

A double decker bus designed to pass under
A low bridge without the roof knocked asunder
Was the challenge set, and a solution found,
But the answer was not quite so sound.

A bus required of lower height and full capacity,
Let's have two levels of upper flooring, what an atrocity!
Passengers could sit upstairs but could not stand aloft,
Slide to your seats after walking down a sunken trough.

But the sunken trough is the sunken ceiling down below,
Passengers had to duck their heads avoiding a blow.
No headroom on both decks, a design catastrophe.
One problem solved but two created, plain to see.

On many a day I sat in this bus on my way to school,
Facing this sign playing with the words like a fool,
'Please lower your seat when leaving your head'
Was one that amused me, it has to be said.

How is it that nature's designs are perfect and true?
And man solves one whilst creating two.
We should all keep our eyes open wide,
Nature has design answers it does not hide.

A driver in a sleepy mode and tiring
Could forget which bus he's driving,
Takes a route with a bridge so low,
The outcome is a terrible blow.

Uncle Charlie, God bless his soul,
Took passenger care beyond his role,
Bringing home a bus of happy day trippers
A scenic route encouraged generous tippers.

He knew the route from his childhood days,
Decided to drive far down these country byways.
Alas, forgot the low rail bridge across the lane,
Reversing the coach back was truly quite a pain!

MEMORIES of YESTERYEAR

Home-made shopping bags of raffia and milk tops,
Strong enough for weekly shopping at the co-ops.
Ration books, little cash, and limited groceries,
Hard times, and money does not grow on trees.

National Milk Bar and British Restaurants met our want,
Blackout, Home Guard, and Pathe News from the Front.
Sirens warn, approaching enemy and later the 'all clear',
Out of shelter, dusted down, 30p* for a pint of beer.

Austere Christmases were challenging times,
Home-made decorations of paper chains and chimes.
Not much room to dress a branch of holly,
The fairy atop was a well-worn dolly.

Freemans catalogues of clothing bought on HP,
Insurance man, rent man, calling weekly,
And 'Scotch' men with their selling strategy
Clothed the street, always smiling weakly.

Ah! Those years of ladies' suspenders,
Brought a gleam in the eye for many old benders.
Long before the mini skirt sights,
Then so grateful for the birth of tights.

Bought your sweets in paper cones,
Before you went into the village 'flicks'.
Made sure you didn't sit next to old Mrs Jones,
She shouts at the screen and waves her sticks.

Do you remember Green Shield stamps?
Empty Mateus bottles turned into table lamps.
Teddy boys and teddy girls,
Exhaling fag smoke in rings and swirls.

TV programmes in black and white
Linked by graceful intermissions,
Time to make a pot of tea or grab a bite
To nibble from the kitchen rations.

TV Station closing down at 10pm,
Weather forecast and the national anthem.
TV aerials, all H shaped, were fixed aloof
to chimney stacks on everyone's roof.

Went foreign in 1970, metric in and imperial out,
It seemed to happen without a shout,
Foolscap paper changed to A4 metric size,
No more chains, furlongs, or pecks, was that wise?

Lots of petrol for a pound in 'seventy-four'.
Buy a new car and watch the beginning of a rust pore.
From the show room to a garage for undersealing,
Due to a re-action by road salt at times of freezing.

Things have changed in recent times at quite a pace,
Wide TVs and plastic items everywhere, even false lace.
Digital technology, international race to conquer space,
But we old codgers can now step back from that rat race,
With gentlemanly grace.
* Today's currency

I MET AN ANGEL

It was early March at the start of Lent,
All church halls closed for any event.
No dancing allowed, no entertainment,
So it's the Miner's Hall and I'll be content.

As I entered the hall the band played on,
Too early for many but not for long.
Live music bouncing from wall to wall,
An ethereal sound in this empty hall.

I looked around and across the hall
An angel sat against the wall.
Will she dance with me? I thought
Of all the steps I've not been taught.

I took the plunge and walked across,
'Like to dance?' my words were tossed.
Will she, won't she? There I stand,
But the angel stood and took my hand.

Dancing is romancing, wrote Irving Berlin.
I held her close, she didn't complain,
We danced so quick, we danced so slow,
I never even stood on her toe.

As the evening wore on,
And we danced along,
The bond felt good,
It felt so strong

This beautiful angel in her flowery dress
Lit up the room as the floor we caressed.
She brought so much JOY to my excited heart,
This angel and I would never part.

Like Cinderella at the Ball,
Midnight brought an end to it all.
We kissed in the street and made a date,
The very next night – never leave it too late!

It's near 63 years on from that night of delight,
And the beautiful angel is doing alright,
A slow foxtrot is rather too fast for us now
With some aching bones and a furrowed brow,

But my love for the angel is still burning bright,
As I think of our dancing on that wonderful night.

GROWING OLD

Growing old is too expensive,
Hair and teeth, eyes and feet,
Creams and potions, belts and seats.

Growing old is too expensive,
Indigestion, aches and pains,
Healthcare costs and keeping sane.

Growing old is too expensive,
Pensions drained, savings spent,
Heading for life in a cold damp tent.

Growing old is quite a strain,
Conned and scammed is all about,
And we're too weak to scream and shout.

Growing old cannot be sensed
By those in power and young at heart
Who fiddle as Health and Care are falling apart.

Growing old is coming soon,
To all who live a healthy life,
Better still, if with your wife.

Growing old is nothing new,
Trouble is, it's back of the queue,
And we're just left to sit and stew.
But growing old is for the few,

So, raise a glass to absent friends.
With aches and pains, few lumps, and scars,
We've all pulled through and thank our stars,
Just hang on in and sup some jars.

PART 2

Observational Poems on Modern Life by An Old Codger

The poems in PART 2 are a personal view of life, politics, and the environment at a time when society is becoming fractured in so many ways, confused, and searching for identity.

We're not meant to consume infinite news, porn and food. We live in an era of too much abundance. This is the modern struggle. There is so much of an abundance of cheap, fake, instant dopamine and meaning. How do you motivate yourself to do the real thing anymore?

Naval Ravikant

OH! FOR A PERFECT WORLD

The recent 'Black Lives Matter' demonstration
Prompted deep memories of visiting one African nation.
Apartheid and life for those who don't fit in
With others who wish to dominate their pale skin.

Arrived in J'burg in '76 on a very sunny day,
Opened my suitcase in the room where I was to stay,
Everything was there except one thing I now needed,
The fundamental advice I had not heeded.

No sun cream to protect my soft welsh skin,
I'll just pop out and buy a tube or even a tin.
A pharmacy was near-by and as I entered in
A large stand of skin whitening creams; was black a sin?

The following day, to the University of Witwatersrand
With my host, to discuss the research I had planned.
At the end of my visit my host was being called away
Apologised that there could be a long delay.

No problem, said I, not wanting a fuss
I'll just go and catch the bus.
I stood by the bus stop but the buses went on by,
A white man was standing at the black man's 'byre'.

On a later tour, I paid a visit to Soweto College,
Equipped by Ford Motor, I should acknowledge.
Before I went to meet the staff assembled ready
I stopped at the door to 'spend a penny'.

'No!' said the Head, 'That one's for the black staff'
If it wasn't the norm, you'd have to laugh.
I saw the townships of Soweto and Alex',
Conditions so bad I became perplexed.

Running to school along the dusty tracks and roads,
All dressed in clean and crisp school clothes,
The thirst for learning by all the young I met
Was something that I will never forget.

We don't own land, we don't own property,
We are just short-term custodians, with a duty
To protect this planet and all who on it dwell,
We have no right to force some to live in hell.

There are good people, evil people,
Lazy people, hard-working people,
For all our races living on this earth
Don't damn the lot straight from their birth.

MESSAGE FOR THE UNITED NATIONS

Instant news from far and near,
Fills our homes with many a tear,
For man's destruction and desecration,
Greed and ignorance and persecution.

Obesity and starvation,
Sit side by side in our world of nations,
Corruption, incompetence, and immorality
Reflecting world leaders' personality.

While conflicts run and people flee
Over land and over sea,
With unknown danger and loss of life,
We can't stand by and watch this strife.

Climate change is reoccurring,
Prompted by our thoughtless erring.
Plastic waste is overwhelming,
Choking our oceans and every living thing.

Noah's Arc as Genesis gave,
Was not built for man to be saved
But all creatures, both small and great,
Next time, fire will be our fate!

However small our island be,
Our voice is strong, and technology
Can help correct our increasing plight.
So, let us re-appraise our lot and fight.

United Nations, now is your chance,
Walk the talk and take a stance.
Nations who can, must help the rest,
Divert your assets, do your best.

No time to waste, no time to argue,
Selfish acts must not accrue,
Heads in the sand and wool in the ear
Will, eventually, cost us dear.

Stop the conflicts, clean our air,
Cancel follies, heal despair.
It's time to act, time to follow,
Time to save their tomorrow!

FOOD FOR THOUGHT

"All is safely gathered in"
A comforting line in a Harvest hymn.
Evensong on an Autumn date,
Time to pause and celebrate.

Voices with gusto thank the Lord,
Organ and choir with one accord
Fill the air with praise and joy,
Barns are full and food to enjoy.

The scent of flowers and ripened fruit
Hangs in the air heated to suit.
Sheaves of bread and lumps of coal,
Reflect the urban work and toil.

Sowers and reapers,
Growers and beekeepers
Display the fruits of all their labours
To their friends and to their neighbours.

The earth needs water and warm sun
In balanced amounts or it's no fun.
What we do and how we live,
What we take and what we give,
Is tipping the scales in the wrong direction,
It's clear to all, we have to take remedial action.

Now Harvest festival is in our supermarkets,
With daily hymns of electronic mush,
All designed to meet their targets,
With world-wide food and bottles of 'crush'.

International food is not for me,
My taste buds ruined by a red-hot pea.
No fresh taste and no identity
From across the world, no locality.

The question now is very plain,
Eat what we grow and control our land,
Or food that comes by boat and plane
And see our earth just turn to sand.

WHO OR WHAT IS A CELEBRITY?

'Celebrity' is bandied about,
But is it really worth a shout?
Let's take a moment to reflect
Who deserves to receive this epithet?

Is it one who saves a plastic football,
Or one who saves many lives each call?
Is it one who lip-syncs an adulterated song,
Or one who nurses patients all day long?

Is it one who can cook and fry,
Or one whose dedication makes us cry.
Is it one who has the 'gift of the gab,'
Or one who creates miracles in the lab.

Is it one who can dance and trot,
Or one sent to places where he/she could be shot.
Is it one who seeks publicity,
Or one who exposes an extreme atrocity.

Is it one with disgusting humour,
Or one who seeks and kills off tumours.
Is it one promoting unsafe speeds,
Or one whose life is meeting other's needs.

Is it one who degrades their skin,
Or one who weekly clears our bin.
Is it one with racial traits,
Or a school cook left washing the plates.

Is it one who fights for cash,
Or one who is always ready to dash
To save on land, to save at sea,
Fight the wind, the waves, for me.

To help my plight I sought the book,
Unhelpful words when I had a look,
From bigwig, big name, personality, star,
But I know who my celebrities are.

BREXIT DEBATE IN PARLIAMENT

September 2019

Let's ask the people, the PM said,
The question's way above my head,
  Do we leave or do we stay?
  We will honour either way.

Oh dear! Oh dear! We are going to leave,
Let's vote again and vote Remain,
But that will be one apiece, I believe,
Oh dear! we'll have to go and vote again.

The nation looks on in utter dismay,
That men and women behave this way.
The noise within beats the noise without,
They jeer, they sneer, and they scream and shout.

What a torrid, ugly, bunch,
As they saunter in after their liquid lunch,
No laws to make, it's just pure flannel,
Because they all come from across the channel.

So, let's Remain and keep life simple
Pontificate, ignore the facts,
A few more Acts are more than ample.

Past PMs and statesmen old
With track records that leave us cold
Interfere with the nation's wishes,
Just stay home and do the dishes.

The world looks on as mother of all parliaments
Fiddles and sinks in its own dire sediments.
They are laughing out loud and falling about
In Brussels tonight, as 'no change' they shout.

Enough is enough, close down the palace
And let the homeless use the place.
Trust and honesty are now lost,
We will never know what it has all cost.
Your last voices have all been sung,
What an example for our very young.

LOYALTY

We have given up our loyalty to the old town stores
As we shop and buy from beyond our shores.
Our fidelity is lost as we now click 'send',
For our local shopkeepers is it the end?

Short-term leases and home craft goods,
Charities and eateries, phones and pubs.
Where's the fresh fish, cheese and ham,
Haberdashers and local lamb?

The town is locked inside a retail stockade,
Supermarkets all around; no fee is paid
To park, or walk too far to collect your trolley,
Come right in and spend your lolly.

These one-stop shops, huge and bright,
Oh! It is a glorious sight.
Music playing, bustling staff and enticing offers,
All designed to bring in the coffers.

Its do-it-yourself in every way,
No need for human contact, even to pay.
Just flash your card, that's what they seek
It tells them what you buy each week.

Your local butcher would know your name,
He may even know from where you came,
But these big boys they know it all,
Your frozen goods and from their Food Hall.

What you read and what you wear,
What you drink and your personal care.
Open all day and weekday nights
They're always there when you snag your tights.

Around the town these tin sheds stand,
Lit up dens advertising their international brand.
Marketing of the highest order,
Standing at the old town's border.

They want our custom, they try so hard,
They even give us a 'loyalty' card.
They sell it cheap and stack it high,
Our town shops' loyalty is pie-in-the-sky.

OUR UNITED KINGDOM

"United we stand, divided we fall",
Sang Brotherhood of Man and it applies to all,
Except our self-promoting politicians
Trying to carve ill-gotten high stations.

"The whole is more than the sum of its parts",
So said Aristotle, wise man of the Arts,
A philosopher, intellect, and revered Greek,
It's someone similar we need to seek.

The current leaders of our three Assemblies
Are creating unrest with their constant pleas,
To take their sinking ships into rougher seas,
Spending tax-payers money on fantasies.

Men and women from all corners of this isle,
Stood side by side and went the full mile.
Gave their youth and gave their life,
To protect us all from evil and strife.

Segregation is what they seek,
Like Cypriot Turk and Cypriot Greek,
Iraq's division of Kurds and Shi'ites,
India's split was an horrendous sight.

Perhaps UN sanctions needed to stop this rot,
Or better still get rid of the lot.
Proud nationalism has its space,
But a multi-cultural island is now our place.

WATCH YOUR POSTURE

"Watch your posture!" came the call,
"You're bending over, you sure will fall,
Straighten up and shoulders back
You're walking like a very old hack."

The reprimand is in good faith,
She's only trying to keep me safe.
There is a pain across my shoulders
But I haven't lifted any boulders.

And bending down is quite a task,
'Help me up', I have to ask.
Slip-on shoes avoid the laces,
Belts away, I'm into braces.

What has caused this situation?
It's the ergonomics of my office station.
Laptops are the curse of posture,
Problems ahead, of this I'm sure.

Look around, we're all bending low
As we walk and tap "Hello",
Or send a Selfie of our morning toast
Which goes out there from coast to coast.

Lowry's matchstick men of old
All lent forward in the cold,
But we lean forward with our phone
Thumbs at pace wearing down to the bone.

Our town centres are in a state,
We no longer communicate
Face to face with a smile and a chat,
We don't even doff our cap.

Curves of spine and rounded shoulders
That are present in many elders,
May develop and persist
Growing up with damaged wrists.

Addiction takes on many a form,
Beware the instant need to phone.
Technology offers many a benefit,
Just keep your posture and stay fit.

PUBLIC TELEVISION

Same old faces, same old chat,
Each one talking through their hat.
Supercilious, over-rated,
Wages, pensions, golden plated.

Public TV is a dying service,
Lost its aim, lost its purpose.
Pushed the boundaries much too far,
Programme content makes me jar.

Cruel talent shows are all the same,
Audiences scream at every name,
Every song, and every dance.
I'm sure they've all been put in a trance.

Chat shows are just one dimension,
Far too many for me to mention.
Plugging a book or a failing production,
Or, perhaps, all just seeking attention.

Celebs turn up to plug each book,
They've just learnt how to bake or cook.
Had a child, must tell my story,
Ghost-written, but I need the glory.

Programmes on cooking, and cooking,
And how to kill yourself by crazy motoring.
Dramas unlit and mumbling speech,
"TV walks" on mountains, on coasts and beach.

Variety is the spice of life,
Monotony just gives you strife.
Search the channels, all ninety-five,
Public service just can't survive.

The axe is sharp and ready to fall,
Equal pay and chance for all
Has cost the service a pretty packet,
Close your ears, expect a racket.

Staff will go but from where?
From the office or those on air.
I have a thought, I have a plot,
Stop the grant and sack the lot.

STATE OF FRENZY

We are living in a state of frenzy,
All around us, it's plain to see.
Chaotic lifestyle and travelling nightmares,
Loss of trust and media scares.

Harmony is in short supply,
Too many urban conflicts fly,
No sense, no reason, nor normality,
Just violent aggression is what I see.

The pace of life is all too fast,
It can't go on, it will not last.
We want, we have, we've lost control,
"Click and Go", we're on a roll.

On-line sales are so attractive,
But beware, it's quite addictive.
Sign the courier's little pad,
Hell! what's arrived just makes me sad.

Fashion in, fashion out, we'll just borrow,
Bought today, superseded tomorrow.
Obsolescence is the game,
Forget the waste, forget the pain.

Apps for this and Apps for that,
We've forgotten how to chat.
Frantic thumbs and selfies many,
Just no time to spend a penny.

The world wide web was meant for good,
But evil hands are all around.
Be alert, be aware, as we should,
Slow down, take care and so stay sound.

BIRDS IN MY GARDEN

The sparrows are here,
Out on a spree.
It's time for a feed
So they seek out the seed.

They jostle and fight,
As they try to alight
On the perch of the feeder,
But can't get it right.

The blackbirds arrive,
There are seeds on the ground.
But they want their fair share
As upwards they stare
At the food in the air.

Can they land on the perch
As it swings 'to and fro',
They guess it's a no
And let it be so.

Pigeons swoop down
With a clattering sound,
And flatten the ground
As they strut all around.

The seeds in the air
Are too much to bear.
They try to fly up as branches are tested

For weight and position,
But fail to achieve a worthy solution
And no satisfaction.

Destruction ensures as shrubs feel their weight,
And delicate plants flattened by their drunken gait.
Seeds thrown down as waste
Are not to their particular taste.

The damage that's caused
By yobbos with wings
Is just akin to our two-legged beings
Who trample all over earth's finest things.

The sparrows return from their nests in the hedge
To fill us with joy as they flit from each ledge.
The blackbirds give thanks as they sing out at dawn,
They all have full run of the garden and lawn.

But where are the vandals so brazen and bold?
They've flown into town where it's not quite so cold.
Food is aplenty as it lies all around
Tomorrow I'll find it all over the ground.

What comes out is what's gone in
But I don't fancy using a 'pigeon bin'.
It's on my roof or on the car,
Under my feet, it's gone too far.
So just appoint a pigeon tsar.

Catch and pluck, add stock to thicken,
They'll go down well as organic chicken.

For our dear creatures great and small
There must be a place for all.
But matters of health in urban spaces
Demands prompt action by those in high places.

MY MEDICAL CENTRE

'I just dropped in
To see what condition
My condition was in'
Sang Jerry Lee Lewis.

Ah! For a Medical Centre like that,
Just drop in and raise your hat,
Take a seat and have a chat.

There's no chat for me or MOT,
No chance of a biscuit or a cup of tea,
Just stressful music and no TV.

Vandal proof chairs in a line,
Not suitable for my old spine,
Sitting here waiting since well before nine.

Have I time to spend a penny?
Or will I end up behind the many
Sitting, waiting, and not much company.

Only one ailment can be aired,
I'll try and raise two, paired.
They say problems should be shared.

Oh! My name's lit up, I have a result
But in which room does he consult?
Is it left or right, at which door do I halt?

As I knock the door, I make a choice,
My back, my bladder, or my creaking voice,
It's the NHS, he'll just prescribe a block of ice.

"How can I help you? Asked the voice.
I pondered the question; I have a choice?
He was searching his computer sitting in a hunch.
"I wondered if I could share your lunch,
I've been sitting out there long in that seat,
I now need something good to eat."

....

Now let's be fair and play the game,
Those wonderful angels, too many to name
Have cared for me, my friends and family,
Day and night carrying out tasks we never see.

Our population is expanding, and so are waistlines
Needing gastric bypasses to stem demands in later times.
A shortage of forty thousand caring nurses,
It's time to open our wallets and our purses.

Where they work and where we're treated
May not be grand and not always heated,
It's the human touch, unselfishly given,
So, raise a cheer for the lives their saving.

STRESS 1 – RUGBY

My stress is rising, Six Nations is here,
Line outs failing and knock-ons, I fear,
Hasty passes, careless kicking,
Collapsing scrums and fans not singing.

Who's the ref? What's his name?
Hope he lets them play the game.
Want no tackles around the neck
Fourth official should improve the check.

Commentators' nonsense,
Just make me tense,
And Half-Time chats
With facts and figures and lots of charts.

Replay videos in the middle of the action,
Is it live or has it happened?
Shots of the crowd cause distraction,
Keep the camera on the action.

My stress is high,
We need a try;
Keep the ball and hold the pack,
Just don't fall, pass it back.

Now run like hell
Your strength will tell.
The try's in sight,
Your line is right.

One last step is all you need,
You've got the benefit of your speed,
Over you go with others on top,
We've won again, go collect the cup.

I'm on my feet and all of a shake,
My stress is high, it's more than I can take.
Six weeks now of 'same again',
"COME ON WALES" and win the game.

STRESS 2 - PARKING

I've bought a car that's quite wide,
Not too high and has a streamline side.
But urban streets in Britain are narrow,
Built for horse, cart and wheelbarrow.

Car parks here are laid out tight
When cars were small, so that was right.
I've taken my ticket I'm required to show
And parked the car but can't open the door.

There's an off-road beast, cattle bar and bumper
And driver dressed in a fur lined jumper,
Stepping down from a dizzy height,
His glistening carriage is quite a sight.

He's in the lift and on his way,
For two spaces he should pay.
White man van has parked my other side,
He's OK, his door runs on a slide.

I mention this nightmare, I'm not a clot,
As I carefully choose my preferred slot.
"Put it there" my wife will declare,
But it's not for me, I'll look elsewhere.

I circle around to find 'THE' space,
My stress is rising at a pace.
My 'Better Half' is giving 'advice',
I try to smile and even look nice.

Stay clear of trolleys left around,
They should be gathered in their pound.
Ah! There's the space, quite remote,
To reach the shops we'll need a boat.

I search around to seek that spy,
The camera set way up on high.
I'm in between the lines I guess,
My wife agrees, I'm full of stress.

This parking business is a racket,
These companies are just making a packet.
They time you out and they time you in,
A fraction over and you've committed a sin.

I leave the car quite secure,
All around I've made a tour.
We walk away as I glance back
Someone has just parked his 'Hack'
In the bay just next to mine,
A rusty shell and outside the line.

Now I'm stressed beyond belief,
I wonder if the driver is a motor thief.
She leads me shopping around the town
She needs some shoes and a party gown.

At last we stop for a cup of tea,
I've had enough of retail therapy.
My stress has really gone too far,
I need to get back to the car.

Where did we stop and leave the car?
Is it near or is it far?
Retrace our steps, shop by shop,
My stress is now well over the top.

We must hurry, time's running out,
"Wait for me" my dear wife shouts
As she drags her bags of shoes and dresses,
Now I'm just totally full of stresses.

Where's my car in this large park?
Too many white cars even in the dark.
My wife excels with such a spark,
"Look for that old rusty Hack"

My stress is such I'm on overload
And I'm over time as we climb aboard.
"Just relax" that's my dear wife's repost,
"And put another cheque in the post".

OUR STREETS

Car off road so back to walking
On quiet streets and no-one talking.
A closer view of the state of our roads,
Tarmac sinking, potholes, and there's loads.

Footpaths covered with moss and grass
Health and Safety would not pass.
The situation has become acute,
Bringing my town into disrepute.

Our roads were built for horse and cart,
Their state now really breaks my heart
And suspensions, tyres and wheels,
Half shafts, track rods, links and seals.

Short-term action using patches,
Rain will seep down at the edges,
A winter frost will do its worst,
Larger potholes, tyres will burst.

Drivers keep alert and taut
On urban roads crushed by juggernauts,
And road signs, lights, and camera traps,
Speed bumps, crossings, and black clothed chaps.

Avoiding potholes filled with rain
Is a must or I'm in pain.
Avoiding young cyclists who weave about,
Dashing around, no bell, no shout.

Like Nero who fiddled as Rome went down,
Neglecting our roads in this dear old town
Will raise the cost, like HS2,
To drive on our roads all flat and smooth.

Short term Councils and Governments too,
Defer each problem by calling for review,
Or setting up a Quango which rarely meets,
While we all struggle with our streets!

SHOULD THE SATELLITES FAIL

All our satellites have been lost
And nations have incurred a terrible loss.
No SnapChat, Instagram, or WhatsApp,
I hear you moan,
Laptops, ipads, Kindles and every phone.

Oh! what will we do with no internet?
We'll all start to shake and work up a sweat,
And have to buy paper, pens, blotter, and ink,
And all learn to write, there'll be a hell of a 'stink'.

I can't hold a pen and my thumbs have worn short,
To sit still and listen I never was taught.
How do you write and how do you spell?
Oh dear! Oh dear! I am not feeling well.

I can no longer book, I'll just have to queue'
My County Council will be in a hell of a stew.
I've lost all my friends from far and wide,
I've lost all my selfies; I've lost all my pride.

How do you talk? I used to mumble,
What can I do? I'm feeling quite humble.
I guess I must talk but I don't know how,
Oh! Just been told that milk comes from a cow.

My office has gone, it's now an 'en-suite',
I cannot text and I cannot tweet!
My floppies' no use and neither my sticks,
Oh! Its letters you send and stamps that you lick.

Conference calls are a thing of the past,
It's onto the train, HS2 will go fast.
My Sat Nav's gone and I've burnt all my maps,
I'll just have to stop and ask local chaps.

I'm up in the attic searching about,
There are boxes up here all strong and stout,
With vinyl and LPs, cines and tapes,
Family albums in all sorts of shapes.

We'll gather around with a good cup of tea,
Dust down the projector, what will we see?
Flickering images of you, or is it me?
"Never NO internet", well just wait and see.

"KIDS"

Am I the only one who goes into a skid?
When I hear a child referred to as a kid,
From the highest in the land
To those who lead them by the hand.

Its lazy talk and a disrespectful call
To use this term for infants, pupils, and for all
Our young folk going through identity years,
Just keep this word for that animal with floppy ears.

It slips off the tongue as a form of disgust,
It slips off the tongue in a flippant thrust
Of demeanour, downgrading and of derogatory tone.
For me, this utterance goes right to the bone.

"Kids" Is not an acceptable term to apply
As the collective sum of our young, I decry,
Sadly, our reference books of words and meaning
Support it's use, it's so demeaning.

I am sure it encourages the young to react
To be referred to so flippant and without tact.
So please drop this slang and give them respect,
Name them who they are, it's what they should expect.

They are children, pupils, students too,
Youngsters, sons, daughters, who
Have hearts and souls but have no tail,
Let's stop this term, let sense prevail.

MODERN TV

They gathered together with their favourite tea,
In the panelled room at half-past-three.
"We have a commission," said the Head of Drama
at the BBC,
"To make a series of murder and mystery."

We've received a story that will meet our needs,
The suspense and intrigue makes a real good read.
So let's discuss our plans for adaptation,
Ready to launch across our nation.

Up spoke the Head of Casting, two sugars no milk,
Smartly dressed and wearing a tie of silk,
"I know the actors best suited to this plot,
Their diction's not good and they mumble a lot."

"I have a score of suspense and tension to deafen the ear,
Added the Head of Music, having sipped his decaf tea.
"I'll drown out whatever they try to mutter,
If they cannot portray the skills they should utter."

Two sugars and full cream milk in his tea,
He's from the sponsors, plain to see,
"We'll want close up scenes of sex and violence
And lots of flesh and not much sense."

The HoD sighed,
"We'll have to simulate the whole film,
The leading man just hasn't got it in him.
The leading lady is really quite slim
And she's not keen to get up close to him."

The camera man suggests his wife can be her double,
She's very photogenic and it will be no trouble.
He's the guy that filmed chimps drinking tea,
Has a wife who meets the spec to a T.

"I'll keep the lighting very low,
The viewers will never know
Who is who and what's going on."
This guy likes his tea with a scone.

"I'll adapt the book so much
The male character will now be butch."
This script writer likes her tea
Loose leaf in a china cup, for all to see.

The Location lady has to ask,
She likes her tea in a one-cup flask,
"You'll want it set in a modern time,
Heaps of litter, empty bottles and loads of grime?"

The Programme Scheduler raises his hand,
He likes his tea from a particular brand.
"I'll take a slot after the watershed
When children should all be in bed".

But they can see it next day on 'catch up',
Before they leave to stand at the school bus stop
And discuss last night's late TV with a friend.
Is TV providing education or a poisoned mind?

Am I the only guy out here
Who despairs at our modern TV?
Every play and documentary's commentary
Is drowned out by unnecessary cacophony.

A story does not need to be enhanced with musical tone,
The storyteller should enhance the listener alone.
Enhance the scene with appropriate musical score,
Not the orator, or the programme becomes a bore.

Let us all hear what is being said loud and clear,
Don't fill each second abusing our ear.
Silent moments are as effective as the spoken word,
"Silence is golden, but my eyes still see."

This quote from the Four Seasons and Tremeloes,
Refers to cheating, a broken heart and other woes,
The line can apply here as I conclude my desperate plea,
I'm being cheated of enjoying the content on my TV.

PLASTIC

Plastic, plastic everywhere,
Raining down from our polluted air,
Floating in our every ocean,
Lying there in every portion.

Plastic, plastic everywhere,
Plastic bags and things we wear,
Plastic windows, plastic chairs,
Even wrapping conference pears.

Wet wipes, toys, cars and boats,
Gutters, pipes, tea bags and coats,
Pens and phones, planes and drones,
Body parts but not our bones.

Polymeric is a curse,
Moulded, folded, smooth or coarse.
Any colour, any shade, thick or thin,
But plastic is not accepted in my bin.

Plastic has become a killer
Of creatures great and creatures smaller.
Twelve million tons each year
Into our seas which we hold so dear.

Plastic turned out every day,
Lies on our earth; we'll have to pay
To clear up this poison with long decay,
Worldwide action, we can't delay.

We've polluted our air burning oil,
Plastic lying all over our soil.
We've created a monster of pollution,
Let's come together to find a solution.

SPORTSMANSHIP?

He grabbed his shirt as past him he tore,
He stood on his foot, that will be sore.
His elbow was high as they jumped for the ball,
Sadly, sportsmanship has died, it's no longer the call.

His mouth is ongoing as he harasses the ref,
Does his coach approve, or is he bereft
By the public behaviour of this overpaid lad?
What an example for youngsters, it's very sad.

The plastic ball, white, light, and so flighty,
Curving, dipping, directed by boots quite unsightly,
Pink! Red! Like slippers I gave my old grannies,
Displaying the brand, their accounts gain more pennies.

He's just dived down the turf 'cos he's scored,
His team-mates pile on top, I'm really bored
With all the histrionics of an excited baboon,
Entanglement takes time, the restart isn't soon!

I look at these antics and the current game
And regret how sport is no longer the same,
Since money has distorted the nature of fame,
From grassroot clubs to the Olympic flame.

The game is fast, the ball is light, the turf is good,
The players are fit, a healthy diet, eat the correct food.
Not the days of leather boots and footballs to match,
Painful to head, hard to kick and slippy to catch.

I now prefer to watch from the comfort of my chair,
The TV takes me down to the action right there.
I cut out the chanting and commentators' critique,
And often tell the referee what I think.

The reward today is off the scale in this vocation,
It has subsumed the privilege of representation,
Some have failed to realise their duty and obligation,
To set a good example for the youngsters of our nation.

VANITY

"Mirror, mirror on the wall
Who is the fairest of us all?"
So runs the Pantomime call.

Gaze in the mirror in the hall
And what you see is not you at all.
Your wedding ring is on the wrong hand,
There's no-one like that across the land.

You'll never see how others see you,
You'll never be that other you,
You may look smart, you may look pretty
But it's not you, that's such a pity.

It's an illusion, a false impression,
That tricks us all, across the nation.
Reflections have made man and beast act like fools
Since water lay on the ground in pools.

There are those who think they're in luck
Since they can afford a nip or a tuck,
Or an uplift here and an implant there,
And a range of potions to enhance their hair.

A morale boost? Or the intention
For those suffered trauma and need intervention.
But others seek perpetual youth to hide decay,
Whilst many young want to look older than their day.

Beauty is not the face in the silvered glass,
Nor does it belong to any one class.
It comes from within, the heart, the soul, you see,
And from innocence, inner peace, and sobriety.

It's said that a camera never lies,
It records the truth, it reads the eyes,
A burst of laughter, or about to sneeze.
It offers a picture of what it sees.

Modern technology can be a curse,
For the truth can now be altered and reversed.
Photography, in all its form, is being abused
To enhance, to trick, leaving you and I confused.

Photography has become the mirror in the hall,
Truth is no longer a virtue we can call.
Vanity is being encouraged from a very young age,
A deeply worrying development for this old sage.

BODY ART

I fail to comprehend
This national growing trend
To cover one's skin
With ink that's needled in.

I don't know what to think
When I see this coloured ink,
From finger tip right to the head
And areas revealed when going to bed.

What is the point of this graffiti art?
Faces and words and a dripping heart,
Flowers and snakes and frightful things,
Monsters in flight with very huge wings.

Sailors came home with an anchor so small
A symbol of their professional call:
Flesh now covered in dense ink like cloth,
An outer surface that will never slough.

Revival of an ancient art is not new,
Rekindled before in the 1600's, that's true.
Even the old Prince of Wales and his Dad
Paid a visit to a tattoo pad.

This body art has many forms,
Celtic, Tribal, and Old School, are some norms.
Japanese have always led the way,
Now our nation's 40% are happy to pay.

Come the day when this fashion dies
'Please remove' will be the cries,
Solid carbon-based ink is used,
If you try, you will be bemused.

Dettol was the old protection
For instrument cross infection.
The NHS will now be overwhelmed,
Dermatologists will all go 'round the bend'.

COMPENSATION CULTURE

Should I follow the trend of our nation
Making complaints and seeking compensation,
Ignoring the facts, putting stress on the work-place,
I'm sure I can claim if I make up a case.

I fell down the step, but I was on my phone,
I slipped on the ice, but I was told stay home,
I missed my plane, but I did get up late,
Hair in my meal, but there're off my old pate.

This old codger has witnessed first-hand this false unrest
And the stress it causes to those doing their best.
It's a selfish act in our selfish world,
Prompted by ignorance, greed, that needs to be told.

There's a growing number in our legal profession
'Chasing Ambulances' is their sole vocation.
Choking our courts with spurious debate,
Stand firm, resist, before it's too late.

Resolving spurious complaints expends the public purse,
Money needed to pay for another doctor or nurse.
Tribunal decisions are costly and unpredictable,
Settling out of court for such complaints is forgivable.

No-one can work whilst looking over their shoulder,
Progress depends on technology getting bolder.
Situations exist or arise, no fault of our own,
Compensation due to hindsight is certainly not on.

Hindsight is fine but that needs no skill,
Nor should it be used to criticize or foster ill.
Foresight's the key in so many a vocation,
It's foresight with hindsight that's the solution.

Complaining nations have lost the plot,
Spoilt, dissatisfied, ungrateful lot.
We must not endorse this egoism all afloat,
Whilst voiceless peoples are being raped and shot.

They have the true right to compensation,
It's another case for the United Nation.
You have the power, the means, the role,
The facts are clear, so go save every poor soul.

FROM THE ORGAN STOOL

Can you imagine being left in the lurch,
Turning up for your wedding at the church,
No vicar nor organist is in attendance
As your day relies on their professional dependence.

Serving in Malta and organist at church,
One Sunday, I found the padre making a search,
Sacred items had been moved on the alter,
Deeply distressed as his voice began to falter.

Looking around with thoughts of evil intent,
Petty vandalism or camper who had no tent.
Who, he exclaimed would do such a thing?
But he had forgotten the Saturday wedding!

A prior meeting takes place to discuss a thing or two,
The ceremony, what they say and what they do,
Time, date, and musical wishes are brought to the fore,
Passed to the organist some weeks before.

The distress couple and family too were rather lucky,
The law requires an island Anglian priest with authority
To attend and witness the marriage ceremony,
But I'm not sure whether he could sing any harmony.

Weddings are normally a happy event,
Expensive these days, heaps of money are spent
On outfits and flowers, presents, and shoes,
Elaborate dinners, video films and evening 'do's'.

Excitement increases as the day approaches,
Arrangements are made to convey families in coaches.
On the day, in Church, the tempo is high
Mother of the Bride and others stifle a cry.

While they wait for the Bride and dad, Oh so proud,
The chat in the pews has a crescendo so loud,
The organist plays softly exposing the chat,
"Eh! What do you think of her mother's new hat?"

Hymns are sometimes strange and sometimes new,
I've played "Crown Him" for one and
"Here we go again" too.
No-one has fainted or cried out 'Stop'
When the vicar asks of impediment or not.

The ceremony over its off to the vestry,
Certificate signed, another entry for the family history.
The organist entertains the crowd, their breaths abated
Until the nod for the favoured piece that's awaited.

The Bride and Groom and retinue smiling,
Walk down the aisle, all beguiling,
The chosen score is a grand affair
Wrapping itself around the happy pair.

Funerals are a solemn affair,
Sadness and loss for all to share.
Music is chosen to respect their desire,
Sometimes the service includes the choir.

It's been a pleasure and a privilege really,
To be part of many couples' holy matrimony
Music is the spice of married life,
Binding together husband and wife.

I'M A VULNERABLE PERSON (Gov. coronavirus)

I am old and vulnerable, as I've been told,
My body's weak, I'm no longer bold.
My faculties are all in decline,
I'm rather like a bad vintage wine.

I have good distance vision, as per test,
But I am not sure about the rest.
My teeth are deserting, but my nose is good,
That helps, for I enjoy my food.

I sleep in parts with commercial breaks,
My joints are stiff and my old back aches.
I have shrunk a little and lost my hair
And it takes some time to drop into my chair

I cannot bend down, or I'll start to sway,
My feet are just too far away.
My shoes no longer seem to fit,
Cushion heels have helped a bit.

There are very few hairs upon my scalp
But they are up my nose, in my ears, I do need help.
The camera is to be avoided,
I look old, decrepit, and very worried.

My writing has now become a scrawl,
Graffiti looks better on an old brick wall.
Watch me walking down the street,
My legs go one way but not my feet.

I don't look back at my old full life,
"You can't remember it" chips in the wife.
I've furloughed now for many a day,
They called it retirement with some state pay.

My filing of papers is quite sublime
But I just cannot find them the very next time.
My I T skills are coming along,
But I no longer can sing a song.

I'll plod along and take my pills
To fend off all those many ills,
I like a nap just after lunch
After I have shouted at that TV bunch.

I am not too old to spot a bias
As media work is a simple science.
Stop putting words into a person's mouth,
He'd turn in his grave would old Lord Reith.

I don't go out far, I never roam,
I guess I would rather stay at home.
There are jobs to do, I have the tools,
But I'm not allowed to stand on stools.

The seasons of the year just come and go,
I can no longer clear the snow.
I have a man to cut my grass quite flat
And one fit chap calls to prune and chat.

The world has changed and changing still,
High spec technology for when you are ill.
Our lives are fast, it's all on a screen,
There's men and women and some now in between.

The birth rate rises every year,
Resources are stretched and very dear.
It's now a case, as a club bouncer would shout,
'It's one in as one goes out'.

But life's been good with little strife,
A pre-war Leo with a Taurus wife,
An on-going successful, handsome, family,
So, I'll just sit back in their glory.

COVID-19 and MY FEATHERED FRIENDS

As we celebrated Christmas with all good cheer,
Families exchanging gifts, whilst some drank beer,
Across the world an elderly couple and son became sick
In the land of the Chinese Republic.

The house sparrows on the bush beside our home,
Were in their usual continuous form.
Constant chirping to find a mate and build a home,
Unaware, like us all, of things to come.

In January, as the 'Martin Luther King' day
Was being celebrated across the USA,
Trouble was brewing in that other far off land,
Human to human transmission happened in old Wuhan.

Ever-hungry pigeons strutted their stuff around the town,
Seeking sustenance from tubs and grub thrown around.
Like them, we had no cares, no consternation,
and life was good,
Jobs and travel, 'retail therapy', education,
and twenty-four-hour food.

World-wide cases began to accumulate,
Action was needed before it was too late.
But it was after Mothering Sunday when it began to click
And COVID-19 was declared a pandemic.

The beautiful blackbird sings on our front gate
At four o'clock each morning and he's never late.
He lifts our gloom with his repertoire and poise,
Indoors, all I hear is procrastination and political noise.

Ignorance is bliss, they say,
For our feathered friends that's true,
But this virus will leave a price to pay,
Did it really come out of the blue?

Its folly to be wise, they say,
Have our experts led us down a way
To deal with this unprecedented entity
And save lives, our health, and our sanity?

COVID-19 – A WAKE UP CALL (Spring 2020)

A bug, we were told, was on the run,
If it reaches UK, it will be no fun.
Countries have closed their entry points,
Cruise ships held at offshore anchor sites

Oh dear! The bug's slipped through,
Does anyone know just what to do?
A Cobra meeting was convened,
The PM spelled out the unpleasant scene.

Experts explained the future scenario,
Infection will rise until it reaches a plateau,
Announcements were made to stay inside
The shut-down is on, it must not slide,

As we began to bunker down,
Was anyone shopping in the town?
Retail and hostelries have closed and so have firms,
The Chancellor has found money, but on his terms.

"Book another home delivery with our store",
Advised the wife as we have done before.
I went on-line and followed the guide,
Step1, book a slot and I abide.

First free slot was three weeks, truly,
We booked our goods albeit prematurely.
Some were replaced or 'out of stock',
But they did their best and delivered on the clock.

'On the front line' has a new meaning,
The enemy, not in uniform, is unseeing.
Our forward troops fight not with guns,
But pumps and tubes to clear out lungs.

Patience is a virtue we need to hold,
Accept advice and do as we are told,
Don't push your luck, so stay at home,
It is so selfish to leave and roam.

Our peaceful country for so many a year
Has made us blasé, at law some sneer.
A wake-up call has now been sounded,
It's time to change, time to be grounded.

So, put away our childish things,
Stop and listen how the blackbird sings.
What possessions do we need?
This pandemic we need to heed.

We are losing the clever, the caring too,
The young, the elder, and not a few.
Our past life now has gone away,
We are going to have a huge price to pay.

COVID-19 and YOU

Beware this microscopic invisible bug,
Stay far away and give no-one a hug.
Like the genie out of the vessel
It's going to cause a great deal of hassle.

It moves around in silent transportation,
On coughs and sneezes, hands, and locations.
If you touch an outside surface, then wash your hands,
So, stay indoors and shelve all your plans.

You're not alone, all humanity's under pressure,
So think of others as they work, I'm sure,
To beat this bug and send it packing,
Expertise and specialist knowledge are not lacking.

Just stay at home and keep yourself fit,
You may have something you need to knit,
Or paint, or fix, or clean, or sew,
Have a garden? Get it ready to sow.

Clean the car in and out,
In your shed just have a rout,
Find those spanners you thought you had lost,
Clean the windows and save some cost.

Write a story or compose a song,
One that we all can sing along,
To cheer us up as time goes by,
We need to laugh not start to cry.

Put things in place in readiness
For when we are clear of all the stress.
Sharpen your tools, or mind, or skill,
Clear your head and don't get ill.

Recovery will come and we will all bounce back,
Ignore the nonsense spouted by TV hacks,
Get prepared to run the mile
And more, with a broad grin and happy smile.

I have followed my own advice,
The old shed door is looking nice,
My spuds are in and seedlings are potted,
Our Home Delivery has been slotted
For three weeks' time and that was the first,
All this work has given me a thirst
But it's all there on that delivery list!
So, I will just have to run the tap,
Stay indoors and be a good chap.

ELEPHANTS NEVER FORGET

Staying at home, day & night, as Boris directed
Will create further problems not expected.
Life in constrained spaces with the wife,
Will surely bring on trouble and strife.

"The mail's arrived it's lying on the mat,
Some are bulky and some are flat."
"Leave it there, Dear, for a day or two,
Otherwise we both might end up in a stew"

"The bins have been emptied and they're in the way".
"Well dip your shoes in the disinfectant tray,
Or leave them outside near the back door.
We both can't have a throat that's sore"

"Now wash your hands, your wrists as well,
With this new virus you never can tell,
Sing the birthday song, and repeat it too,
Then 'Pen Blwydd Hapus' loud and true."

"Oh Dear! My cupboards are bare and so is the freezer,
Book a delivery with that supermarket geezer."
"There's no available slot, dearest, until the Fall,
Someone has bought the food, the shelves, and all!"

The internet and world wide web
Will solve our plight it has been said.
But local shops have come to the fore,
Just as many were 'on the floor'.

Elephants never forget and neither should we,
When this pandemic is over, and we are free.
Here's a new strap line we should follow,
SHOP LOCAL FOR THEIR TOMORROW.

I'M IN LOCKDOWN

I'm staying at home and washing my hands,
It's a peaceful time across our lands.
The sky is empty, the roads are quiet,
But I'm not happy with this new etiquette.

I'm 'confined to barracks' or is it 'open prison'?
Faces call to check my situation,
Food parcels or things from Amazon arrive
To keep me sane and keep me alive.

I guess its rather like boarding school,
As I must not break any rule.
Stay alert at every lesson,
The Head directs our daily session.

There are regular updates with graphs and charts,
It's a mathematician's lesson on analysis and stats.
The Head or deputies provide the class with fiction,
Or is it literature with jargon about prediction?

Questions from the class are invited
But dumb-head media with brains blighted,
Waste time, do not listen, and in a provocative stance
Create mischief and trouble; I look on askance.

The Governing Body is never united and forward looking,
Despite their establishment's deep peril and financial sinking.
Ah! It's our history lesson to be learned
Of Nero, who fiddled while old Rome burned.

We have been in a 'bubble', my wife and I,
For many weeks, time really does fly.
It's of bricks and mortar with the odd stud wall,
But the P M's new 'bubble' may burst and re-infect us all.

I'm getting ready for our eventual release,
Will school-runs fly by and hot heads shatter my peace?
Will facemask wearers be friends, or do I call the police?
Will my streets be covered in Autumn leaves or slippy ice?

Will the world be the same, or is this the chance
To end all anger, greed, cruelty, and malice?
The world can be closer without the travel,
Will this land of beauty before our eyes unravel?

MASKED INTRUDER

Mask on face, this decrepit Lone Ranger,
Walked in, a desolate stranger,
The lass at the till looked quite askance
She knew I wasn't there for a dance.

Shoppers stood still, baskets in hand,
My mask was black, and I felt grand.
Three ply and soft, over my mouth and nose,
I looked the part from head to toes.

As I strode down the aisles,
I sensed no smiles
The shoppers stepped back as I walked past,
Thinking how long their lives will last.

I whipped out my wallet and my card,
The lass at the till tried very hard
To slide the goods across the beam,
I was the first she had ever seen.

She filled my bag with extra care,
This codger had only eyes to stare.
I swept the reader with a manly flurry
And left the shop in quite a hurry.

I heard a distant sigh of relief,
The lass thought I was another thief.
The shoppers wiped their sweating skin,
What was it that just came in?

No smoking gun nor buckskin fringe,
No spurs or whip to make one cringe,
Just a face mask stark and black,
Created havoc and a near heart attack.

This situation may well soon change,
Compulsory face masks of fashion and range
Will have to be worn by one and all
When visiting any shop or stall.

You wear a tattoo or metal nose ring,
False eye lashes or some hoodie thing,
So what's the issue with a mask?
When carrying out a shopping task.

Face masks are the gas masks of yesteryear,
As an old codger I've now worn both in fear.
Thick rubber, all encasing, so heavy to wear,
Three ply cotton, so light, I know which I prefer.

So, keep your chin up - under cover!
Even if you're with your lover.
Stop the spread of this dam bug,
And soon we'll meet and have a hug.

LOVE ONE ANOTHER

This dear Old Codger has had enough,
COVID-19, 'house arrest' and all that stuff.
Decided to stretch his legs and walk
Down the drive, anyone out there able to talk?

His car looked all forlorn and in quite a mess,
Choosing white was not a good idea, I guess,
Out came the hose with soap-filled brush,
The birdlife around went into a hush.

The call went out, a brisk "Coo" all commanding,
"Plant Busters' crew to assemble for urgent briefing",
So, all perched in comfort but always alert,
The Squadron Commander arrived, looking rather pert.

"Tonight's target has been set in place,
Remember, when you go in, this isn't a race.
Number One will strike at six,
Hit the target, I want no tricks.

Stacking above in their military grey munition,
These elite war machines moved into position.
Down they go, hit after hit, the damage is seen
On the roof, the bonnet, and glass windscreen.

Returning to base on a neighbour's roof,
Billing and cooing and strutting aloof,
The Commander assesses the number of hits,
The poor Old Codger will have a hundred fits.

The old lad refreshed from sleep and rest,
Takes a stroll to see his car at its best,
Like Joseph's coat, things have gone too far,
He finds he now has a multi-coloured car!

Out came the hose and soap-filled brush,
The enemy is hiding in a nearby bush,
The car is washed, the old man breathes a sigh,
"Ah well, thank goodness cows can't fly."

'Love one another with a pure heart fervently....'
S. S. Wesley's church anthem is sung frequently,
And was sung by the Old Codger when he was a lad,
The message is strong, stay safe,
And of your good health be glad.